T0088132

LYONS ON
HORSES

LYONS ON
HORSES

His Proven Conditioned-Response
Training Program

John Lyons
with Sinclair Browning

Skyhorse Publishing

Skyhorse Publishing books may be purchased in bulk at special discounts for sales promotion, corporate gifts, fund-raising, or educational purposes. Special editions can also be created to specifications. For details, contact the Special Sales Department, Skyhorse Publishing, 307 West 36th Street, 11th Floor, New York, NY 10018 or info@skyhorsepublishing.com.

Skyhorse® and Skyhorse Publishing® are registered trademarks of Skyhorse Publishing, Inc.®, a Delaware corporation.

Visit our website at www.skyhorsepublishing.com.

10 9 8 7 6 5 4 3 2 1

Library of Congress Cataloging-in-Publication Data is available on file.

Cover design by David Ter-Avanesyan and Adam Bozarth

Print ISBN: 978-1-5107-6767-6

Printed in the United States of America

Contents

Introduction
by Rick Lamb

*I*t's been more than a century since the first Model T rolled out of Henry Ford's Piquette Avenue plant in Detroit and put the working horse on the road to obsolescence. Yet, the horse is still here, happily serving us in perhaps its most important role ever: as a counterweight to the stress and complexity of modern life. For all its continuing popularity, the horse remains a mystery to most humans. Those truly smitten want to unravel the mystery, and that's where John Lyons comes in.

He's not the first or only teacher of horsemanship to gain favor with the public. In fact, there is a long tradition of horsemen who have achieved a measure of fame and fortune by teaching people to train their own horses. Still, John Lyons is special.

He's special because he's a thinker as well as a doer. He's special because he's a maverick who doesn't mind shaking things up a bit. And he's special because he is relentless in his pursuit of perfection, wherever that leads him. Perhaps most important, John Lyons is special because he inspires trust. "America's Most Trusted Horseman" is more than a marketing handle; it reflects how legions of horse owners really feel about the man.

The trust is well-placed. You see, John's highest priority, as evidenced in the first of his Three Training Rules, is your *safety*. It's easy to get caught up in the pursuit of lesser goals, goals that are meaningless when a rider's confidence has been shattered by injury. John doesn't fall into that trap. You feel safe and empowered with John from the beginning. If he were a doctor, you'd say he has a great bedside manner. He has a kindness about him, a strength, and a quick smile. Best of all, he has time for you.

The day I met John Lyons is seared into my memory. It was 1998 and John was already a superstar in the horse industry. He headlined at horse expos. People waited in long lines to meet him and buy his products. Major corporate sponsors courted his endorsement. I, a rookie radio host little known to him or anyone else, was going to convince him he should partner with me on some audio books.

John made time for me. At our breakfast meeting, he was cordial, a bit more reserved than I expected, and very businesslike. I sensed immediately that this would be a hard sell. And why not? John had his own little empire going, with books and videos and saddles and bridles and logo wear and events. He was known as much for his business acumen and work ethic as he was for his way with horses. John Lyons probably didn't need audio books—or me, for that matter. Still, he must have heard something he liked because after a few thrusts and parries over the financial details, he smiled and shook my hand. We were officially partners. A few months later we were in the recording studio, me prodding, John explaining, and the light of understanding in my brain beginning to flicker on.

What emerged from the recording session was "A Conversation with John Lyons," five double audio CDs that captured a good-sized chunk of John's training philosophy and a few of his favorite techniques. Along with the audio books emerged a new John Lyons fan. Me.

It's not that I disregarded everything else I was learning on my horsemanship journey. It's more that John filled in the gaps and gave me valuable tools and perspective on the whole matter. I believed then, and still believe, that John's work can be taken as a whole or cherry-picked according to what you need. I've found it to be very compatible with other humane, empathetic, psychology-based approaches to handling horses.

In the sense that he understands, respects, and uses the horse's nature as a unique animal species, I consider John to be a "natural" horseman. I know he doesn't care much for the term. It has spawned a fair amount of misunderstanding and oversimplification. Still it does separate horsemen such as John from those who don't bother with why a horse behaves as it does, and for that reason, I find the term useful. What you call John isn't all that important—what you get from him is.

So what can you really get from John Lyons? How about a proven way of reaching your goals with horses, a way of finding the joy you envisioned when you began down this path? And here's a little bonus: What John teaches has broad application. It's the marriage of common sense and science. It's the secret to influencing the behavior of any living creature. Although I'm not a dog trainer, I suspect that one could easily adapt John's methods to that species, or to alpacas, or hamsters, or children.

A few years ago, I interviewed John in front of a live audience at a horse expo in Oregon. We had one hour, sandwiched between other presentations on the expo schedule, and the printed program listed a specific topic—weanling training—for our interview.

The seminar room was packed. John walked in as I was setting up my recording equipment on the front table. Immediately, a lady in the first row asked him a question about training her grown horse. John began talking. Five minutes passed and I was ready to start the interview but by this time, John was on a roll, perched on the front edge of the table.

I fidgeted, coughed, and noisily rearranged the mic cables. Nothing. John kept talking. That's when I realized that he was in *the zone*. I'd seen this before. It's this place John goes where time stands still and all that matters is the teaching. The audience didn't mind. They were loving it. Another ten minutes passed. I fidgeted, coughed, and rearranged some more to no avail.

Finally, with nearly half of our allotted time gone, I stood up, put my hand gently on his shoulder, and said, "John, I really hate to interrupt, but we need to get our interview started." He looked at me in surprise. I think he'd forgotten I was back there. I heard a couple grumbles from the audience as John came around and took his seat, but once the interview picked up steam, everyone was onboard. It turned out to be another classic John Lyons radio interview. Shorter than I'd planned, but great nonetheless.

It's this single-minded dedication to helping people with their horses that defines John. I've referred to him several times as a teacher. That's how he sees himself, and he takes full responsibility for making his subject comprehensible to the student. It's no coincidence that he sees your role with your horse as that of the teacher, too. In the land of Lyons, it's the teacher's responsibility to break things down as finely as needed for the student to learn. John does that for you so you can do it for your horse.

And right there is perhaps one of the most important themes to emerge from this modern revolution in horsemanship. The horse is perfect as God made him. If a partnership is going to exist between this exquisite prey animal and the planet's ultimate predator, the human being, it is up to the human to orchestrate that relationship, to earn the horse's respect, preserve his trust and develop the level of communication needed for the job. That means making a plan and working the plan. Can we do this without losing the horse's natural perfection? John Lyons thinks so, and he's dedicated his life to sharing with us his way of doing that.

You are in good hands, my friends.

Have fun and ride safely.

Rick Lamb

Rick Lamb
TV/Radio Host and Author
The Horse Show

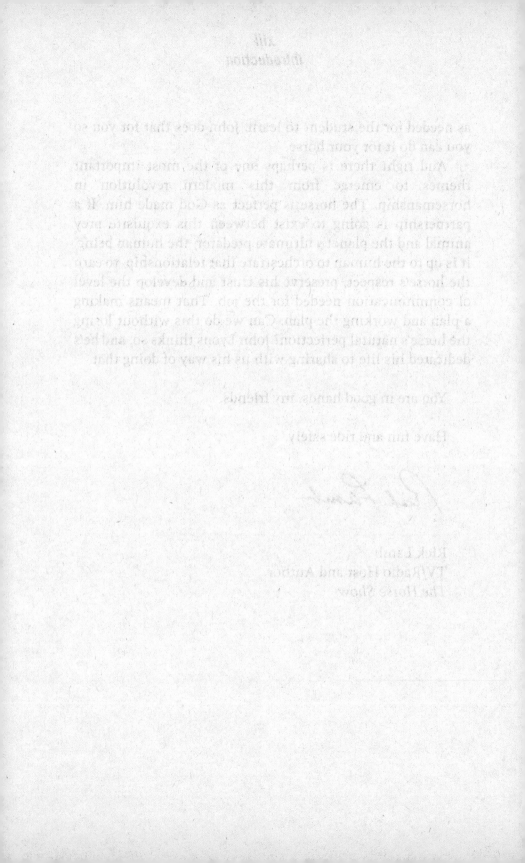

Foreword

J ohn Lyons doesn't believe in miracle workers when it comes to training horses. He doesn't believe in equine swamis or horse gurus, and he doesn't want a psychic to tell him what his horse is supposed to be thinking. What he does believe in is using a reasoned, logical approach to horse training. He believes the horse is a conditioned-response animal, and all of his work is based on the use of common sense and logic.

John's training method is distilled from his years of giving clinics throughout the United States and Australia. The clinics were limited to ten horses and were open to all breeds and all styles of riding, as well as to any type of problem horse. Horse owners, on arriving, would explain what they wanted of their horse, and John agreed to satisfy their wishes or the clinic was free. He never turned away a horse or rider. Working in a limited time frame, with horses he had never seen and did not know, kept John striving for better training methods and solutions. His experiences in dealing with over two thousand horses have molded his unique training program. Today, most of John's teaching is done in symposia that are geared toward larger audiences—fifty to three hundred people—who follow the breaking of only one horse.

I first saw John Lyons at a clinic he conducted in Tucson a few years ago. Typically, he congratulated all of us for coming out on a cold morning to see what a "turkey from Colorado" had to say.

Well, I didn't see any turkeys that morning, but I did see a philosophy that so impressed me that it has had a profound effect on my dealings with horses ever since.

John doesn't like it when people say he's special. But he is. When you see John work with a horse you feel that something extraordinary is taking place between man and animal. More importantly, John is a special teacher.

This book might be better titled *The Friendly Lyons,* for it is an instruction manual in using friendly persuasion in teaching our horses what we want them to do. His methods do not include force.

But I'm getting ahead of myself.

So I went to the clinic and found myself mesmerized. Especially when John slipped the bridle off his stallion, Bright Zip, and the two of them began working an unbroken mustang mare who happened to be in season and was feeling friendly. In spite of her flirtations, Zip ignored her, and within two hours, John was riding the wild mare.

I returned home and played a little with my own horses, trying out some of John's training suggestions. And I watched for the next John Lyons clinic in Tucson. The following year, I went back.

After attending the second clinic, I decided that since the round pen was such an important part of John's work starting colts, I needed one. I bought a pen and began working my own horses. After a few weeks, I decided that I wanted to test John's system, which I had seen him apply to wild horses, to see if it would really work for someone else.

I put out the word that I was looking for a wild horse. Within a week, I had a pasture-raised, wild-as-a-March-hare three-year-old filly in my round pen.

Now the real fun began. Not wanting to waste any time, I went to work, following the steps John had demonstrated at his clinic. Several old cowboy friends gathered to offer advice.

"We'll hold her down so you can get a halter on her." "Rope her." "Where's your snubbing post? You need a snubbing post!"

The comments were as cheap as well water. But the filly and I ignored them and continued our work.

Now I've got to tell you that I had worked a wild horse years ago. I did it the old gentle way. I tried to lure her with apples and carrots, and I sat in the corral for days before the horse would come anywhere near me. I talked to her, sang to her, whistled, and begged, and it was still weeks before she didn't dash off whenever I got within ten feet of her.

But this time, following John's instructions, I was petting the March hare within three hours. Petting her entire body! And the cowboys were scratching their heads and saying, "Tell us more about this guy from Colorado."

Inspired by my own success with the March hare, I contacted John and suggested that we collaborate on a book. I knew that if I had success with his training methods, others would too. And so will you, if you use the principles and lessons included here. It's that simple.

An exciting aspect of John's training is that it will work on any horse or mule, regardless of its breed, age, sex, temperament or previous experience. Over the years, he's worked with unbroken mustangs from the Bureau of Land Management, Olympic event and dressage horses, five-gaited Saddlebreds, hunters, jumpers, Peruvian Pasos, Thoroughbreds, draft horses, mules, Curly's, Australian stock horses, as well as all of the common breeds. His methods will also work for any discipline—English, dressage, or western.

We've all read books where you need an overly complex schematic to train your horses. Frankly, I have trouble remembering all that stuff, so it was a real relief to learn that John believes in the K.I.S.S. method. Keep it simple, stupid.

Lyons on Horses is a progressive training program in which you master one stage before moving on to the next. John breaks complex assignments into segments, or segment-goals as he calls them, as he gives us an opportunity to learn the art of horse training. Realistically, a lot of you will pick up this book and thumb through it, picking out only those parts you are particularly interested in. That's fine. With one major exception: breaking colts.

Finding trainers who will break colts is getting harder and harder all the time. Now, with the lessons in this book, you can break your own colt. For your safety, it is important if you are working with an unbroken horse that you follow the instructions in the "Round-Pen Reasoning," "Facing Fear," "Sacking Out," and "First Saddling" chapters before you get on the horse for the first time.

As we wrote this book, we treated the lessons like *Sunset* magazine recipes. While we don't have a test kitchen, all of the lessons in this book have been tested. On horses. By me. I know John can do them. It's his training program. But we figured if I tried everything out, as written, we could see where the writing fell short, or where we might need to explain something in a little more detail or a little more clearly.

To give you an example of how our "test kitchen" worked, after we wrote the trailer-loading chapter, I used John's system to teach a confirmed bad loader to trailer. It went like clockwork except for my stupidity. I was so intent on having the horse get into, and out of, the trailer that I didn't pay attention to our six feet, and one of my toes got stepped on and broken. Now we have a line in the trailering lesson cautioning you to watch both your feet and the horse's.

We want this to be a messy book. Underline those passages you think will be especially helpful to you. Commit John's three training rules to memory, for they will serve you well in evaluating *any* training method. Take the book out to your round pen or corral and use it as a hands-on aid as you train your horse.

Finally, I want to tell a story on John. I went to a horse show with him one day, and he turned my perspective around 180 degrees. At previous shows, I would ask myself, "What is that rider trying to get the horse to do?"

After listening to John for a few minutes, it quickly became apparent that he saw the horse show a bit differently. The question he was asking was "What is that horse trying to tell his rider?"

Looking at the participants from this viewpoint really opened my eyes. Horses with wide-open mouths were in effect saying, "Ouch, get off my face." The horse that was dancing around its owner, who desperately wanted it to stand still, was asking, "Do I really have to stand here and take this?" A Prix St. George dressage horse, with arched neck and tucked head, was pleading, "Please give me more rein." John pointed out that that particular horse was probably originally trained western. The signs of miscommunication were everywhere.

I said earlier that John Lyons is a special teacher. He is. Through the lessons in this book, John teaches all of us to look at horses in a new way, to approach our training in a new light. With his instructions we will be safer and calmer in our training. We will not only become better communicators with our horses, but we will also become better listeners.

I think I can speak for all of us who read this book, when I say, "Thanks for sharing, John."

Sinclair Browning
Tucson, Arizona

LYONS ON
HORSES

Chapter One ━━━━━

My Philosophy on Horses

I want my horse to be my partner. To me, that means someone who helps me, who isn't a nuisance, and who makes my job easier. Someone I can trust and who trusts me; someone I don't have to force to do something.

In order to have a true partner, I have to let go of him and trust him. As I let go I have to understand that he's going to make mistakes. I don't need to reprimand my horse for his mistakes, instead I need to show him why I want him to do certain things. I know that if I can avoid fights with him, I'll end up with a better partner.

In many ways, dealing with horses is a lot like dealing with kids.

There are times when in order to teach them you simply have to let go. For instance, a lot of people want their horses to stand by them or to follow them, but they never let go of the reins. If they do and the horse walks off, they're inclined to think, "What a dumb horse; he has to be tied up!" If I let go of my horse and he takes off, I think, "I'm a lousy teacher." His walking off tells me I need to teach him more in order for him to stay with me.

If I can't get my horse to overcome a problem, it's my lack of knowledge, not the horse that is at fault. If I can't get him to load in a trailer, it's not because his eyesight is bad, or that his mother was an Appaloosa, or that he's having a bad day, it's because I haven't taught him right.

If you see a problem in a horse, or a training area in which he needs improvement, don't ignore it. For instance, if you have a head-shy horse you know that overcoming this problem is a priority before you attempt to mount him. If you don't correct the problem, you run the risk of being injured or even killed if you accidentally get close to his head. In such cases ask yourself which training problem comes first.

If the horse is afraid of being tied, you need to take care of that problem before you put him in a cross tie. If you take him to a horse show, someone who doesn't know better might tie him, and while you're off collecting your ribbon, he's causing a major wreck. Suddenly things that don't seem so important can become terribly important.

I don't care what the horse has done before or what's happened to him. From here on out we'll deal with today only. We can't change the fact that someone may have hit the horse over the head five thousand times, or that little kids may have thrown rocks at him. There is no way any of us can change what has already happened, so it's futile to spend any time thinking about the horse's past experiences. It's his problem *now* that's important, not the history of the problem. Sometimes we get so involved with that history that we can't concentrate on correcting the problem.

The past can also cloud our thinking as we begin making excuses for the horse's poor conduct, rather than asking the horse to change his behavior.

The horse is a very adaptable animal. He is fully capable of changing his behavioral patterns, especially if he is given time to make his own decisions.

I personally don't believe any horse is either vicious or beyond being able to be trained.

Horses are never too old to learn or to change bad habits. The good thing about a horse is that whatever behavior we'd like to change, we can. We don't have to accept any behavior from the horse that we do not like. We just have to concentrate twice as hard on training him to do those things we want to, to get him to change.

A woman came to one of my symposia and said she had waited two years before trying to change her horse's behavior, because she didn't want to do the wrong thing. Don't be afraid of making a mistake with your horse. We all do. And we're all forgiven. The biggest mistake is to succeed at doing nothing.

The bad thing about a horse is that everything I like about him today probably won't always be there, unless I continue to practice the things the horse is doing that I like. I also never want to lose sight of the fact that my horse is always learning.

You must decide what it is you want your horse to do. Obviously some breeds do certain tasks more gracefully than others. A draft horse or a Thoroughbred can do a sliding stop, but neither does it as prettily, or holds it as long, as a horse that has been bred to do it. My point is that all horses are capable, to some degree, of jumping, sliding stops, barrel racing, trail riding, or any other task you wish them to perform.

PREJUDICE, AN UGLY CONCEPT

Prejudice is ugly in any form. There is not one breed of horses that is better than all others, or one best breed. Each has been bred for specific characteristics. A Paso Fino is not bred to pull a heavy wagon, few draft horses compete in calf roping, and a Quarter Horse is not designed to run a hundred-mile race. But there are more differences within a breed, than between breeds.

A good friend of mine, Tom McNeil, taught me a valuable

lesson about prejudice. He never, ever, said a bad thing about anyone's horse, even if they begged him to.

After I bought Zip, I called Tom. I told him I'd bought a stud. He was really excited and thought it was great. Then I said Zip was an Appaloosa. Dead silence invaded the telephone line. I waited. And waited. Finally a low, weak voice responded. "Well, I've known two good Appaloosas," he sighed.

He had to dig deep. But even if he didn't like Appaloosas, he wouldn't say anything bad about them. This is a good lesson for all of us.

ATHLETES IN ACTION

The horse is extremely versatile. Because he is capable of executing over 108 different movements, even the very best trainer on the best-trainer horse will still get less than thirty percent of the horse's potential out of him.

Can a horse canter backward? A man named Blackburn had his horse doing it in the 1860s, and on the correct lead! Can you get your horse to swish his tail on command? Scratch his ear? Lift his lip? Roll over? All on command? Probably not, but the horse has no problem at all doing these movements on his own. Trainers don't teach horses to do sliding stops and rollbacks. That's ridiculous. Horses can already do everything we get them to do. A two-day-old foal can slide and roll back. In our training, we're just trying to say, "Remember when?"

A CONDITIONED-RESPONSE ANIMAL

My method of training is based on building control over the horse through reasoning with him. And I want to be in control one hundred percent of the time.

The horse is a conditioned-response animal. We set up a condition (kicking with our right leg), and we get a response (he picks up his left lead). If we set up the condition often enough, and we get the same response consistently, then the condition becomes a cue for a specific, desired reaction or response. This is the cornerstone of my training program and will be repeated often throughout this book.

We must remember that the horse doesn't understand right or wrong. I often hear someone say "the horse is in a wrong lead." The horse doesn't know he's wrong.

Ninety percent of successful horse training is in correctly defining a problem. By dissecting the problem, we'll be breaking it down into very specific parts. My impatience has taught me to put steps into the teaching process. Most of us learned to write the letter *A* in steps: We were taught to first make a slanted line, and then another, and, finally, the cross line. To make the entire *A* at one time would have been too much for a small child's mind. The same is true in training horses. As we go through the exercises in this book, you will find that they are broken down into segments, small steps to be accomplished on our way to reaching our designated goals.

Throughout our training, we must never fall into the trap of thinking that we are tougher than the horse. Even the scrawniest seven-hundred-pound horse is capable of inflicting great, even mortal damage to any man pitted against him. So during our training, we'll be working with safe ways to teach the horse, where we'll be in control.

THE THREE TRAINING RULES

Since there are as many training techniques as there are trainers, I established the following rules for evaluating any training procedure. I strongly encourage you to apply them to any method, whether it's mine or someone else's, that you choose to train your horse.

1. The Training Must Be Safe for Me.

A training procedure isn't any good if you or I end up in a hospital. We are more important than any horse. The horse may not mean to hurt us, but he is so big and strong that he may not be able to help it.

I always tell myself the horse I'm working with today has no more value than any other horse. A free horse and a million-dollar race horse are treated exactly the same way. They can also do the same amount of damage. Your or my little finger is much more important than the million-dollar race horse, so the training techniques we use must insure our safety. Accidents will happen, but we must, and can, minimize the danger. We also need to listen to ourselves and remember that every time we put ourselves in danger, we are wrong.

2. The Training Must Be Safe for the Horse.
So what if we can force a fractious horse into a trailer if we have to have him patched up by a vet when we get him out of it. The technique is of little use if the horse needs his head stitched, or he breaks a leg. We'll take as many precautions as possible for both ourselves and the horse.

3. The Horse Must Be Calmer After the Lesson Than Before It Started
This is the horse's way of telling us that he understands and is comfortable with what we are trying to teach him. It's important that the horse remains calm throughout the training process. Pain distracts. The more pain you inflict on a horse, the less he'll be able to concentrate on what you're trying to teach him. If I ask you to solve a math problem and then slap your knuckles with a ruler, could you concentrate on my question? The same is true of a horse being jabbed with spurs. Pain gets in the way of learning and should be avoided. If a horse is nervous, he's telling us that he's not sure of what we expect of him.

A calm, responsive horse is the best proof of the success of our training, much more so than a wall full of ribbons. The behavior of a horse in a show reveals just how well the trainer is doing. If the horse performs well it is because he understands the lessons that the trainer has taught him and he is comfortable responding to the trainer's commands.

My Philosophy on Horses

THE BASIC CHARACTERISTICS OF THE HORSE

While we're teaching our horses, we must never forget the four characteristics of the horse, for these will influence not only his behavior, but our teaching methods. They are listed here in order of importance:

1. The Fear/Flight Instinct

The horse is not a predator. His natural instinct is to run, rather than fight. This means that if he is startled or is afraid, his most immediate reaction will be to run, to try to escape his concern. His fear will take precedence over everything else. We can understand this, because when most of us are afraid, we want to get away from the thing that's scaring us.

Since we can't possibly get a horse used to everything in the world, we need to approach his fear and teach him how to deal with it. We can't tell the horse not to be afraid, because that request would be unreasonable. But we can teach him what we want him to do when he *does* become afraid.

If a horse is reacting out of fear, then we'll treat him the same way we would if we found a lost five-year-old girl crying on a street corner in a big city. Would we yell at her to quit crying? Tell her to shut up?

No. We'd try to get her to relax, and we'd try to build her confidence. That's the same way we'll treat the horse if he is fearful.

Bear in mind also that there are some things that your horse should fear, but may not. For example, he may go up to a rattlesnake and stick his nose into its face. All this means is that he doesn't know that the snake is dangerous.

2. The Pecking Order

The horse's social framework is highly structured. Horses are herd animals. This is a very important influence on a horse's life, for it starts from the time he hits the ground as a foal.

If we watch horses in a pasture, we'll see a dominant animal push another around the field. That lead horse may want to stop moving, but he can't because the dominant one won't let him.

Just as each horse has his place in the herd, you'll have a place in your horse's social order. To the horse, you are not a person, you are just a two-legged animal. If your horse bites you, he's telling you that you are lower in the pecking order than he is. Whether or not he bites us is dependent upon his perception of where we fit in his social order. Just as he will bite one horse and not another, so he will bite one person and not another.

Other signs that the horse thinks he is above you in the pecking order include: walking all over you when you're leading him, crowding you into a gate, walking off when you're saddling him, throwing his ears back at you, kicking, or turning his head elsewhere when you ask for his attention.

Don't worry about establishing dominance over the horse, just make sure you get the right answers to the questions you ask. The important thing is not that we think we are higher in the pecking order, but what the horse thinks.

For instance, if the horse steps on our foot, we'll slap him and make a big ruckus so the incident is not pleasant for him either. When something becomes important to you, it becomes important to the horse. If it's not important to you, it will never be important to your horse.

We need to crawl inside the horse's mind to tell him that we're higher in the pecking order than he is. We can learn from watching other horses in the pasture how they establish their order.

If we put ten unfamiliar horses in a pasture, the only way to find out who is the dominant horse is to put out a bucket of grain and watch to see who gets it.

Most horses pair up. As they do, one of them will become dominant. Rarely would the #1 dominant horse in a herd pair up with the second most dominant. For the purpose of illustration, we'll say that the #1 horse has paired with the #5 horse, that is, the fifth most dominant of the herd. He is not friendly with #2.

When the #1 horse, the dominant one, walks over to the feed bin, poor old horse #2 is saying, "Uh-huh, I better get out of here, here *he* comes." As horse #2 walks off, what is horse #1 saying? "Ho, ho, I *am* the toughest! I can control any horse here. I rule this herd." This is a positive reinforcement for the #1 horse, a negative reinforcement for #2.

My Philosophy on Horses

When new horses are put together, there's usually a lot of squealing, striking, nipping, and kicking, but after the pecking order gets worked out, then horse #1 doesn't have to be quite as violent in his reign.

Now if we take a grain bucket into the corral, and the #1 horse comes up to chase the #2 horse off and we are in the way, what will happen? If the #2 horse thinks we are below him in the pecking order, the chances are good he'll bump into us, kick at us, or in some other not-so-friendly manner tell us to get out of his way, or else. If, on the other hand, he perceives himself as being below us on the pecking order, then he'll probably show us respect and get out of our way.

Since the horse is always learning, we need to be aware of what our actions are teaching him. For example, let's say I'm feeding my horse. He is on the other side of the corral as I walk into the pen. I walk to the middle of the corral and set the feed bucket down, then turn around and begin walking toward the gate. The horse begins walking toward the feed bucket as I'm walking away. What am I teaching him?

Is he thinking, "Here comes old John. He's such a nice old guy, he's gonna feed me." Or is he thinking that I'm leaving because he's #1 and that he is chasing me away from his feed bucket. If I don't want him to learn this, then I'd better make sure that when he comes up to the feed bucket he comes with a good attitude.

We need to recognize this characteristic of the pecking order in our horse because it is of paramount importance in our relationship with each other. Never let your horse come up to the feed bucket with a bad attitude. Remember, what your horse knows has been ingrained in him for thousands of years.

3. Laziness

A horse will usually take the road of the least amount of work. He's basically lazy. Just like you and me. If you were given a choice between digging a ditch with a teaspoon or a shovel, you'd choose the shovel. Now if you were given the choice between digging with a shovel or using a backhoe, I'm sure the backhoe would be the winner. Finally, if you had the choice between the backhoe, or not digging the ditch at all, I feel certain the ditch wouldn't get dug.

This characteristic relates to horses as well as to people. If you give a horse a choice between not moving and moving, in most cases, he will choose not to move. So our first step in training will be getting the horse to move. We must have movement in order to train him. Once we have movement, even if it is wrong, it can be redirected by setting up either easier or more difficult circumstances, depending upon the response we want. If a horse trots when I want him to walk, then I'll practice a few trotting exercises. I'll trot him a few steps, turn him left, trot a few more steps, turn him right, back him. Pretty soon the horse will think, "Gee whiz, I just wish he'd let me walk."

4. *The Reproductive Instinct*

Unlike either mares or geldings, stallions have a built-in drive to reproduce. God said to the stallion, "You have a reason to be on this earth. You need to reproduce by mating with mares."

If we were to take down all the fences in our vicinity and turn loose a gelding, his main concern would be eating and sleeping. He'd walk around thinking, "Dum, dum, de, dum, time to eat," or "Dum, dum, de, dum, time to sleep." Chances are good he'd not stray very far to pursue either of these endeavors.

If we turned a mare loose in this same fenceless country, she'd spend her days eating and sleeping too. But some days she'd be grumpy, other days she'd want to be loving a stallion to death if there were one around, and at other times, she'd want to kick his everloving head off. So we could say, at times she'd be less content than the dum, dum, de, dum gelding, and if she's in season, she might be grumpy and, therefore, not quite as willing to respond to our commands.

Now we turn the stallion loose without fences. He'll eat. He'll sleep. Because he has to. But most of his time he's going to spend walking, walking, walking, looking for that mare that God sent him down here to meet. He'll walk all of his life searching for her.

We can learn a lot about our stallion by watching him in the pasture. Is he rearing? Is he jumping everything in sight? No. Who tells him when it's OK to breed? The mare. She controls that stallion miraculously without a lead shank. Why can't we?

This reproductive drive is behind many of the stallion's behaviors. If a stallion wants to put all fifty mares in a corner of the pasture, he can do it even if he's not the #1 horse there. Why? Because he has the drive to do it. If we recognize this, we can then deal with it in a logical manner. We'll teach the stallion when and where to use this inner drive, when it's OK to breed, and when it's not.

Because of the stallion's strong purpose in life, we'll need to invest more time in his training. It may take us two hours to train the gelding, five hours to train the mare, and twenty hours to train the stallion. While we'll be able to put any of them in a pack string, if we're in a hurry, then we'd better train the gelding.

It's important to remember that age, breed, sex, lineage, and experience do not affect any of the horse's characteristics. They are endemic to all stallions, all mares, all geldings and should be considered any time we are planning our training program.

THE THREE ASPECTS OF A HORSE

When we are considering training the horse, there are three additional aspects that we must consider: his physical, mental, and emotional capabilities. Our progress in training is determined by our horse's area of slowest development. A letdown in one area is similar to the weakest link in a chain.

First consideration is the physical. Our horse must be physically able to do what we're asking. A six-month-old foal, for instance, is not physically ready to be ridden, although he may be mentally capable of learning cues. While we can do many tasks with him, such as leading, loading in a trailer, or ponying, he is just physically incapable of being ridden at this point. Size isn't everything, for a 16-hand two-year-old may be able to be ridden, even raced, but he may lack the coordination, or the physical maturity—for example, he may have open knees—to barrel race or do a lot of mountain work. While most horses can be trained to perform most tasks, again, physical abilities must be considered to get the best possible training results. For instance, a short, low-hocked horse may be more *physically* suited to cutting cattle than a 17-hand long-legged warmblood, who, in turn, may be more physically suited to stadium jumping.

Next we must consider the horse's mental comprehension. Does he understand what we are asking him to do? This is where our schooling comes in. We must be sure we are explaining clearly to the horse what we want him to do, and that he understands it.

Finally we must consider a horse's emotional state. Does he show persistent signs of nervousness or fear? Does he seem unable to relax? Does he go to pieces under pressure? If so, we will give him exercises and cues that will help him control his emotions. We will need to get him excited and then calm him down. The more practice we give him, the calmer he will become.

There is always an answer to a training problem. Whenever I run into a problem I always review the rules, the characteristics and the aspects of the horse for insight and for a possible solution.

Armed with this knowledge, we're ready to begin training.

WE CAN ALL BE TRAINERS

First of all, be assured that, given the desire, you can train your horse. You don't need to be a professional. Persistence overcomes fear and impatience, and teaches us how to handle our frustrations.

Getting good results with your training is not just luck. When someone ends up with an extra-intelligent horse, that means that there has been a lot of hours of practice involved.

A little girl climbs all over her horse, and he stands still. By her attention, she's training him to do just that.

Many times an owner training his own horse will actually do a better job than a professional, because the owner will take more time with the animal.

We see this all the time. An eight-year-old girl whipping the socks off a pro in the show ring, because she's spent hours and hours with her horse. The girl and her horse are so closely knit that if she got on another horse, she wouldn't know what to do.

My Philosophy on Horses

But on her own, the sky's the limit.

The training methods outlined in this book will work for all horses and all riding disciplines. The dressage horse changing gaits at different letters of the arena, is no different case from the Quarter Horse going around trees out on the trail. You, the rider, are still learning that you're asking the questions late if the horse misses a letter in the dressage ring, or a bush on the trail.

Most of the training exercises that follow will take minutes, not hours or days. None of them is hard. All they take is practice. You don't need a master plan. You can go out and enjoy yourself on the trail, where you'll be training your horse and no one riding with you will know you're training.

Training should not look like training. It should look as though the horse and the rider are playing together. For instance, you can trot your horse to a certain point, raise your seat off the saddle and ask him to stop. If you do that fifteen times during a trail ride, the horse will stop any time he feels your seat rise. This will not only make your horse lighter in his stops, it will make you safer, for every time he feels you leave him, he'll stop.

Any training procedure needs to work one hundred percent of the time on every single horse. If it doesn't, then the horse is telling us that this program isn't the one we need, because it won't work on all horses. We'll need to look for a procedure that does.

I need to solve riding problems from the horse's back; manners will be taught from the ground.

A good training method will work on either a dumb or a smart horse. A good training method is a good training method. Period.

Conversely, if some training procedure has failed once, it's apt to fail again.

If you pick up the reins and your horse does nothing, he's telling you one of two things: "It's Tuesday, and I never stop for anyone on Tuesday," or "What? I don't know what you're asking me to do."

The horse is a conditioned-response animal. If we set up a condition often enough, and get the same response often enough, then the condition becomes a cue. Remember, there are only two reasons a horse doesn't respond to a cue:

1. He doesn't understand it. Mentally he does not compre-
    hend what the cue means, which means we haven't taught
    him well enough.

2. He understands the cue but chooses to ignore it. He's
    choosing to do what he wants, rather than answering our
    request.

Whatever our horse's reason for not responding properly to our
cue, the solution is the same. We must return to a place in the
horse's training where we can set up the condition and get the
response we want.

Sometimes we make excuses when our horses won't do certain
things. I've heard a lot of them. "My horse is blind in one eye."
"He's a Thoroughbred." "Yeah, but his mother was head shy."
The list goes on. We'll take the blind horse as an example. Just
because there are things that that horse doesn't know, or cannot
see, is no excuse for his misbehaving. In fact, there's a blind show
horse in Phoenix who does quite well, and the owners never tell
the judge he's blind until the class is over. But that's another story.

All of these rationalizations that we offer for our horses, are just
excuses for our lack of ability to train them. I'm a trainer. Either I
can get the horse to do things, or I can't.

There aren't any mental problems, only behavior problems.
Lineage, conformation, whether the horse has won two thousand
trophies or none, whether he's one year old or twenty, none of it
matters. Either we can get him to do what we want, or we can't.

Training a horse can be compared to baking a cake. If you put a
pan of flour in the oven and cook it for an hour, you'll get
something that doesn't even look like a cake and sure doesn't
taste like one. Then you make the cake, using all of the proper
ingredients, but you add a pound of salt. Now you've got
something that looks like a cake, but tastes like a salt lick.

My point here is that training a horse, like baking a cake,
requires the combination of many ingredients to produce a
successful result. Just love, or just love and patience will not work
by themselves. We must add additional ingredients in order for
our training to be successful.

Some of the additional ingredients that must be brought to the
training process are logic, knowledge, respect, and yes, temper.

Sometimes we need to lose our temper in order to overcome our fear. Also, it is not always wrong to hit a horse. Sometimes it's right. This might be a good time to discuss the three-second rule.

THE THREE-SECOND RULE

While we're talking about losing our temper, I'll tell you about my three-second rule.

The horse never ever has the right to kick or bite you. Biting is more dangerous than kicking because it is a more aggressive act on the horse's part. You can't ever justify that action in your mind.

I don't want to be bitten. If the horse tries to bite me, I try to *kill* him. His act is that dangerous, and my rule is that simple. I have three seconds in which to *kill* this thousand-pound beast. The only limitation I'll put on the murder, is that his head will be off limits. Remember, I don't want to blind him, I want to *kill* him. Immediately after I've exhausted the three seconds, I'll pet him to reassure him that I still like him, but he knows that he made a *serious* mistake that almost cost him his life.

The word pet is important here. Pet, or rub, or stroke your horse. Do not slap him. Slapping is an aggressive gesture to the horse. Also do not lightly touch the horse. Horses are ticklish and find this annoying. Remember to always pet and reassure the horse after you have invoked the three-second rule.

This rule can be used any time the horse is biting.

COMMUNICATION

Some people think horses are dumb. Ability and intelligence are in all horses, regardless of breed. Their so-called stupidity stems from our poor communication. Training a horse is like drawing a picture. The better I draw the picture, the better the communication. If I'm drawing a horse in pencil, I've communicated something. If I add crayon to my drawing, you can then tell that the horse I've drawn is a Palomino. Does this mean that you've gotten smarter? No. It means that I've become a better communicator.

It's funny, but I find that when I get better at communicating, my horse gets smarter.

Communication means dealing with specifics. And the specifics must be broken down into steps. Many people do not want to do the simple things first. That's what sells bits. People buy and try different bits in order to get their horses to stop. A stop is built up with many smaller exercises, all of which must be performed consistently before a nice stop can be achieved.

I don't believe in using any restraints other than a halter. That's all I'll use, for I'm not going to let my horse teach me that I have to hurt him in order to train him. Also, before I can control my horse, I have to control myself. Every time I jerk on the reins, or spur him, I pay for it with unwanted behavior on my horse's part.

When I talk about restraints I'm including tie-downs, draw reins, martingales, lip chains, and twitches. Any restraining device is a gimmick. A gimmick forces a horse, rather than teaches him. Such devices are aids that don't work very well for very long. Some people think that all they need is one magic gadget or one special exercise to get their horse to do a manuever that required hours of practice of a horse handled by a trainer.

It doesn't work that way. If we're restraining our horse with gadgets, we're squeezing him into a mold. And what happens when we take the horse out of that mold by removing the gadget? We're back to square one with the horse still tossing his head or not carrying it in the right position. I believe there are more reliable ways in which to get better results. Training techniques need to be backed up by common sense, logic, and reason, not gimmicks.

I think of my training as a game between me and my horse. The horse's part of the game is that he says to me, "Oh, John, I'm going to make you pull on my mouth to slow me down." My part of the game is to figure out a way I can get him to slow down without pulling on his mouth. If I pull, he wins. If I don't, we both win.

When teaching, we must always question ourselves to make sure we're explaining what we want so clearly that the horse does not misunderstand us.

It's important that we not ask the horse questions that will result in incorrect answers. If we ask, and the horse doesn't do what we're asking, then either he doesn't understand the question, or he's telling us "No, I don't have to." When he does that, we are establishing a pattern of refusal. We need to watch this. If I keep saying whoa, and my horse keeps moving, then he's learning that "whoa" doesn't mean anything. The way for him to learn is by my asking, and his doing.

If we're getting the proper responses, then the horse gets into the habit of doing just what we ask him to do. It's like dealing with our kids. Sometimes we get into the habit of saying no to them. We'll be reading the newspaper, and they'll start to ask us something, and we say no before the question is out. Only after the question is finished, do we realize that it required a yes answer.

We need to quickly learn how to present things so we get the right answers. We need to ask those questions that make it easy for the horse to answer yes. The way I know if I'm asking yes questions is if the horse does what I am asking. I will not ask anything of the horse unless I'm pretty sure I can get it.

Remember, if we set up the condition often enough, and get the response often enough, then the condition becomes a cue. If you teach the cues for a specific response, then the horse will respond that way in any situation. You won't have to blame the horse's acting up on his environment.

There's a word game that I play in the symposia that illustrates this principle. It probably won't work on paper, but I'll include it here so you can try it on some poor unsuspecting soul. Spell the word silk, three times fast. Then, as quickly as possible, ask, "What do cows drink?" The answer will most likely be "Milk." What did I do here? I tricked you into thinking my way.

The concept here is that we can get the horse answering questions the same way, get him to start responding to us in a manner that gives us the answers we want. When we do that, we are conditioning his mind, so it's important in our training that we get consistency at one step before moving on to the next. If we are having trouble getting that consistency, then we must go back a step to the point where we *can* get the horse to respond consistently.

As an example, let's say we are working a horse in the round pen. We will start by having him move. That's all we want and that's all we will work on at this point. Once he is moving consistently (step one), we will go on to the next step (step two): having him move to the left. Once he is moving (step one) consistently and to the left (step two) consistently, then we will add another step (step three): changing direction. Only when the horse is doing the third step consistently will we move on to the fourth, and so on.

THE IMPORTANCE OF GOALS

No introduction to a training program would be complete without mentioning goals.

We all have goals we want to reach with our horses and we understand that with time and effort we can attain these goals. Too often, however, we start seeing problems develop with either our horse's behavior or our own tempers. We become frustrated because we're not reaching the goals we set out to achieve. As trainers, we must know we are progressing, or we'll become anxious and begin pushing too hard in our training sessions. Our anxiety will result in bad habits for ourselves and our horses. It's important to remember that the horse is a definite mirror image of his owner. Nervous people make nervous horses.

Set daily goals when you ride; reasonable goals that you can reach today in your training. Be specific about what you want to achieve, and always work to improve your basic cues. When problems do appear, return to a point in your training where you have control, and begin from there. In practicing this, you will always be positive with your horse. Remember, the secret of the ballet is to perfect the single dance step.

The key to improvement is not always additional knowledge, or more sophisticated training methods. We need only to strive to improve what we are already have accomplished, to perfect what our horse is already doing. This is the secret of almost all successful trainers.

Almost anyone can ride his horse and get him to turn and to stop. Getting the horse to do these simple manuevers when, where, and exactly how we would like, can be a challenge. The art of dressage is based on this simple ability to control the horse so that he and the rider become one. If you want to improve your horse's performance, don't overlook the basics, because that is where the need for improvement lies.

We should also remember that it's important that we enjoy our horses. It's OK for our horse not to know, or to do, everything. He doesn't have to know every leg cue, or have a perfect head set, in order for him to be safe for us to ride. Setting too many goals can exasperate us and ruin our trail rides. Or we'll come back to the barn after a pleasant ride, then work on things until we get frustrated. Suddenly horseback riding isn't any fun anymore.

We should also realize that we all have different needs our horses fulfill. A horse does not have to ridden to be worthwhile. Some people can just pet and feed their horse, and that gives them satisfaction.

I know a lady who sits with her horse while he eats. She watches him and listens to him chew his feed, and she gets tremendous satisfaction from just being with him at mealtimes twice a day. That's all right too.

Most of us need to realize why we have horses. Less than one percent of us will earn a living with our horses. The horse is basically a recreational animal, so he should be enjoyed. When we find reasons not to ride him, then he isn't doing what he's supposed to do, and we should sell him and buy a book about horses—it's cheaper.

We talk about goals because they help us keep our perspective and help assure us that we are achieving something. Goals keep us from becoming too critical of ourselves and of our horses. Goals will show we're improving, and this improvement will, hopefully, stem frustration. If we don't see improvement, then something's not working.

Setting a goal will help determine a starting point. By defining both our goal and our starting point, we can determine if there's a hole in between the two. Since the goal is the finish line, we can't start there. Once a starting point is set, we'll break down the process of getting to the goal into steps. As we go into this breakdown, we'll constantly be asking ourselves, how can we make it simpler for the horse?

During the training lessons in this book, we'll be breaking our goals into smaller and smaller steps, or segment-goals.

MOTIVATION

Coupled with the learning process, we should consider motivation. Motivation is the basis for all learning, for all change.

Everything starts with motivation. Motivation gives you a reason to change. The reason to change precipitates change, and once change is accomplished, you've learned. If you've never built a house before and I put you up on a Colorado mountaintop and say, "Build one," you may shrug and say, "He's crazy, I've never built a house before in my life." Now if I take you up on that mountain and say, "You might want to build a house before the first snowfall since you're not coming down until spring," then I'll bet, in spite of your never having built a house before, you'll be out gathering materials with which to construct shelter. That's motivation.

The horse, too, must be motivated to learn.

TIMETABLE FOR TRAINING

We need to realize that training takes time. It takes consistent riding over years. To turn out an all-around horse, one that you can rope on, ride and do ranch chores with, takes many hours of riding on the horse and exposing him to many different situations. If you're inconsistent in your training, it will take twice as long to get the results you seek.

The same is true of the pleasure horse. To have a horse that will trailer, will be calm in all situations, will travel well uphill and down, will cross streams and travel cross country, takes many hours of riding.

Most people set unreasonable timetables for themselves and their horses for what they want to teach them. Thus, they become discouraged and believe they are not good trainers. In getting into the habit of wanting to solve problems quickly, we sometimes work too fast. If we get excited and put pressure on the horse, we are limiting ourselves, and, at the same time, the horse may start developing unwanted behavior. We need to relax and take our time. Most problems don't need to be solved in a day, or in three days.

It's not how much time you spend with the horse, but what you are teaching him. A month is a long time if you are constantly training. Some horses will make major strides, say in backing or in circling, in just one day. So you can actually spend just a little time with a horse and accomplish a lot.

Horses, like people, vary in their learning speeds. Some horses need more time, some less. Techniques can be taught over several sessions, or over several days or longer, with excellent results.

Also, the following of my three training rules will affect training time. Any time you think that either you or the horse is in danger of being hurt, back off.

Variety is important at all stages of training. The more diversity that you can add to a normal training session, the fresher the horse is going to be. Asking a horse to do many repetitions of any one exercise at any one time is going to: (1) cause the horse to begin making mistakes, which will irritate us and cause us to irritate him, making his performance fall off even more, and, (2) cause the horse to become fatigued. So break things up. If you are working a reining horse, turning him and spinning him, go off and trail-ride him a bit and then return to working on circles for a few minutes.

Midafternoon and evening are not good training hours. These are siesta times for the horse, his natural resting periods.

There will be times when we're training the horse when he will get excited, but this shouldn't last more than two or three minutes. The horse is fighting to understand what we want him to do, or is fighting the lesson. This stress should be momentary, and shortly you should see a major improvement in the horse's behavior. He'll start to calm down and relax. Immediately after, say, rearing, he should get better at the exercise he was doing before the flare up. If he doesn't show this improvement, then open up and give him more room. You need to go back to that place where it was simpler for the horse to be right. Take a step backward.

Trail riding is an important component of training. Once a

horse can be ridden, one of the most valuable training areas we have is the open trail. Not only can a horse get sour and lazy in a training ring, but even after years of training in such an enclosed area he may still be unsafe out in the real world. Opportunities for lessons abound on the trail, so don't overlook this important aspect of training.

Finally, don't get discouraged. People will say, "My horse has only one problem." I've never seen a horse that has only one problem. My own don't. Even world champions have problems. Problems usually come either in pairs or great big bunches.

Frankly, I don't know when we, or our horses, quit learning. The more training we give our horses, the better they will become.

HORSE PSYCHOLOGY

Horse psychology is really popular right now. The horse's mind is important, but it's not everything.

The horse is a lot more talented than we think. I get scared sometimes because I don't know what they're thinking, or how much they really do know.

One time in California there was a man who was having trouble with one of his studs. He tried everything to improve the animal's behavior, and finally a friend suggested they call a horse psychic. This was the same lady who talked to the great race horse John Henry, years ago.

When the man finally relented and they called the woman, she apologized and said she was terribly busy and couldn't come out to his place. She asked if there was a way she could talk to the horse on the phone. He said there was. She suggested that he take the telephone and place it up to the misbehaving stallion's ear, and in that way she could talk to him.

Feeling somewhat sheepish, the man traipsed out to the barn, portable phone in hand, and held it up to the horse's ear. After some time had passed, he asked the woman, "Are you done?"

"No," she replied, returning to her conversation with the horse, who, as near as the man could tell, was saying nothing.

When they were finally done talking, the woman told the

horse's owner, "You have two studs. You like the other one better, and this stud is jealous. He tells me he's already bitten off one of your fingers, is that true?"

The shaken man confessed that, yes, it was.

"Well, he tells me if you continue to pay more attention to the other stud, he'll bite off another."

I don't know how this story turned out. I only know that it emcompasses entire areas of the horse that I not only don't want to think about, I don't want to know about. If a horse psychic wants to talk to my stallion, Zip, I'm saying no!

Chapter Two ━━━━

Round-Pen
Reasoning

*T*he round pen is a specific training tool that we use when training our horses. Before working in the round pen, it's important to read this chapter in its entirety so that you won't hurt your horse. Working in the round pen is the start of controlling something the horse does, and sets the foundation of our training process.

The round pen should not be used to exercise the horse or to longe him. It is a teaching tool and should be used accordingly. If, during my training program, you need to have the horse in the round pen, this will be indicated in the explanation of the training procedure.

I do little or no longeing with my horses. I would rather teach a horse to obey than wear it down. Also, the purpose of the round pen is not to get the edge off a horse, because that just gets harder and harder, and takes longer as the horse becomes more fit. If, however, you feel safer longeing your horse, there is nothing wrong with it. From a practical standpoint, all horses should longe, simply as a soundness test.

The round pen will give us the ability to gain control of our horse, without being connected to a thousand-pound animal that may hurt us. That's a lesson I learned from my horse Zip. He taught me that when I have him attached to the lead rope, he's also got me.

Every time we try to confine, tame, or lock up a huge beast, the wrecks will get bigger and bigger. If we have fixed objects, such as a snubbing post, around us and the horse, we are in more danger than when working him in the open. The same is true with runaways. Most of us can stay on a running horse and be in little danger. If we add trees, and fences, and other perils to that equation, then we're looking at a potential wreck. If we confine the horse, we're confining ourselves.

The round pen is also a good place to work a horse that has never been handled, as well as one who has learned to fight any person who comes within a hoof's reach. Working in the pen will get the horse's attention, which we must have in order to teach him anything. If a student is sleeping in math class, even with the best teacher in the world, how much can he learn? The same is true for the horse. We not only need to get him in class, but we must have his attention.

The horse can't ignore us in the round pen. He'll gain an attitude of listening, and his attention span will increase. If the horse is listening, the teaching is easier, and he will want to get along with us once he finds out that we're in control. The round pen will also help a horse regain a positive attitude toward learning. If we can stop him from questioning us, he'll do what we want.

When we ride the horse in the round pen, he can't run away

with us. Since we won't have to worry about where he's going, we won't have to pull on his mouth, and we can concentrate on his training.

We'll actually use the pen very little in our horse's life. The ground work training will be done here, as well as our first ride or two.

We'll use the round pen until we are confident the horse is responsive to us, and until we are reasonably sure we can control him. This will be anywhere from three to five days, depending upon how intensively we are training.

For a wild animal, or one that hasn't been handled very much, the round pen will be a very important aid in beginning training, for again, it is one of the safest ways we can get the horse's attention.

Like all of the training discussed in this book, this lesson will work for any horse or mule, regardless of sex, breed, domesticity, temperament, or previous experience. The round pen is also a valuable training tool to use on any new horse we may acquire, as it helps us recondition the horse to respond to us, instead of fighting or ignoring us. If an older horse has developed a poor attitude, usually it is because the horse has been conditioned not to respond to his rider and has repeatedly gotten away with unwanted behavior. The round pen is a safe place for the rider to gain confidence as the horse develops his attention span. If after working on a pattern of response on the ground with the horse in the round pen, we then climb on his back and ask him to move forward, he will be much more likely to respond correctly.

In Chapter One, we discussed a horse's social life and his pecking order. Now we'll put this to work for us here in the round pen, for it's important that the trainer outranks the horse in the horse's mind.

I call this the hammer and nail relationship. Whenever two minds get together, whether it's two people, two horses, or one horse and one person, one of them is going to be the hammer, the other the nail. The hammer will always make the final decision. Either you will be in control, or it will be the horse. Which one is the hammer will not be a secret, for you will both know which one of you is in charge.

The instant that you lose control, the horse already knows it. Conversely, if you know you've gained control, you'll have that knowledge an instant before the horse. It's that simple.

Since the basis of our training program is to have control of the horse one hundred percent of the time, it's important to make sure you are always the hammer. Working the horse in the round pen will be a good basis for establishing this control.

THE PHYSICAL ROUND PEN

If you are constructing your own pen, begin with a fifty- to sixty-foot diameter. I lean toward sixty feet. This is a small enough area that you can comfortably work a horse from the ground, yet large enough that a big horse can lope easily. If you go any larger than sixty feet, you'll lose control, as the horse can run over to one side of the pen and stop.

If the round pen is too small, the horse will have a tendency to challenge it. A wild horse that is being worked in a smaller pen, will feel territorially threatened and will have more of a tendency to jump over or through the fence.

It's also harder to get the horse to move in a small pen because he feels he doesn't have any place to go.

Remember old pi from high school? To translate diameter into circumference, multiply your diameter by 3.14 (pi). Roughly, a diameter of 50 feet = 157 linear feet; 55 feet = 173 linear feet; 60 feet = 188 linear feet.

Solid-wall construction is the best, of either wood or metal. The type of material is not as important as its strength. With a solid wall before him, the horse will think much less about running through or over the fence. The walls should be straight, not slanted, and should be built solid from the ground up to six feet. A horse will rarely think about jumping over a fence of this height.

Another advantage to the solid-wall construction is that if your leg is smashed against the wall, the pressure will spread out over ten to twelve inches, whereas with a pipe pen, the pressure against your leg is intensified by being spread over only a two-inch pipe.

Pipe has other disadvantages. The bottom of the horse's legs can hit on the posts as he runs around the pen. Also, if you are riding the horse, your toes may have a tendency to get caught in the support pipes.

The ground in the round pen should consist of four to six inches of good, loose footing. This can be a combination of good soil, sand, and shavings. Compacted soil can cause damage to legs from repeated impact on the hard surface.

If the soil is too sandy, the horse will tire and will have to rest frequently. As the tendons become tired and lose their elasticity, they can tear away from the bone, causing damage such as bowed tendons. Again, the tendons are more apt to tire when the horse is working in sand.

Do not bank the dirt in the round pen. We'd rather have the horse running level so his inside shoulder doesn't drop and he doesn't repeatedly pound his inside front leg.

ROUND-PEN LESSONS

Some of the lessons you'll be teaching your horse in the round pen include:

1. Turning and facing you
2. Standing by you
3. Paying attention to you
4. Trusting you
5. Accepting a saddle and rider calmly
6. Basics of ground-tying
7. Standing still while being mounted
8. Overcoming his fears, such as head shyness or having his feet handled
9. Spooking in place; turning and facing fearful objects rather than running away
10. Developing coordination over ground poles
11. Crossing plastic and other obstacles such as bridges, etc.
12. Developing a positive attitude toward responding to your requests

If you don't have a round pen, or access to one, you might check around the area and see if you can lease the use of one for an hour or two a week. If this isn't possible, you might want to consider boarding your horse for a month at a facility that has one.

While a round pen is nice to have and makes our job easier, I'm not in the business of selling them. If you do not have access to one, you can use a longe line and common sense and still do all of the training outlined in this book in a thousand-acre field.

TOOLS FOR THE ROUND PEN

My training program is not based on equipment, so you won't need to bring a whole lot of tools into the round pen the first time you work your horse. Bring your brain first. Remember that the best training tool in your barn is at the end of your arm. After that, you might want to wear comfortable clothing. You'll need a lariat or a longe whip. I use a calf-roping rope, soft lay, thirty feet in length. The diameter can be anything that feels comfortable in your hand.

You might want to have a jug of water left outside the pen. You can give the horse a drink, but don't give a hot horse a lot of water. Follow your veterinarian's suggestions on how much water, or how little, your horse should have when he's hot.

Ideally you will want to put bell boots and splint boots on the horse's legs. This protective gear will shield him against injury should he crash into the walls or rails of the round pen. A hard bump along a leg or coronary band may cause a crack in the hoof that will last for life. If you can't handle the horse well enough to put on the leg gear, don't try.

The horse will be working loose, without a halter or any other headgear.

BEGINNING IN THE ROUND PEN

We'll begin by asking the horse to move. In a sixty-foot pen, you are always twenty feet away from the horse. You will ask as softly as you can. For a wild horse in the round pen, the raising of your hand may be enough to get the desired movement. If you're working a horse that has been handled quite a bit, obviously you may have to make a little stronger request, for he won't be afraid of you. With the calmer horse, you may have to take your coiled lariat and slap it against your leg, or even throw it in the direction of the nonmoving animal.

The times I've put myself in the most danger were with horses that didn't want to move. They are also the hardest to train. The reason for the danger is that you have to get closer to them and be more aggressive. It's important even with the nicest, sweetest, calmest horse on earth that when you ask him to move, he honors your request. You must establish a pattern of asking and getting the right response. You must get the horse moving around the pen.

It's important that when you ask the horse to move, he honors your request.

Two choices cannot be made. You cannot keep the horse from moving, and the horse cannot decide not to move.

While you can't stop the horse from moving, you can control

his movement. Whenever the horse wants to move his feet, you can't stop him. You *can* control the direction in which he moves, when he can stop, how long he runs, and the gait at which he runs.

Once the horse realizes you are serious about making him move, he has several choices. First, he can run over you. Although this choice is very rarely made, be prepared for it and have your coiled lariat ready to clobber him in the nose, or anywhere else, to discourage this avenue of escape. You must control the horse, just as you must control a drowning person. The first lesson in a lifesaving course is to control that drowning person so you aren't dragged under the water. The same is true here. Control the horse so he does not run over you.

The horse's second choice is to stand and face you. Again, this is not a legitimate choice. The horse cannot say, "This is Friday, and I'm not moving." If the horse doesn't move, do whatever it takes, whether it's throwing the lariat in his direction or even hitting his rump with the rope, to get him to move.

To keep the horse moving, you may have to continue these same tactics. Once he continues to move on his own, stop the harassment.

Finally, the horse can run away from you. This will get him moving, which is exactly what we need him to do, in order to begin exercising his brain.

We will be running the horse at the canter. He can't breathe as well at this gait as he can at the trot, and he will tire more quickly. We'll be using his body to work against him. When the muscles and lungs ache, the horse will begin thinking, "How can I get out of this alive?"

Once the horse is moving, pay attention to his attitude. If the horse comes at me too fast, I don't like it. I want him walking toward me with respect. If he comes in snorting, I'll throw the rope at him and tell him, "I don't like the way you're coming at me."

If you think the horse may try to go over the fence at any time, back off. Backing off can be as simple as letting him slow to the trot from the canter. If he goes over the fence, try to learn from it. The way I look at it is, I'm sure glad he did it now, and not when

I'm on his back. If I caused his going over the fence, then I need to consider why.

If the horse goes over the fence, retrieve him and begin again.

IMPORTANT CONSIDERATIONS

When working your horse in the round pen, there are several variables you will want to keep in mind.

First, you must consider the heat. If the outside temperature is above ninety degrees, then you need to keep that in mind, for the horse may quickly overheat. There are three physiological components to remember when working horses in the round pen. They are:

1. The horse's lungs. This will be the first part of the horse's body to be damaged.

2. The horse's legs. Recognizing that not every surface is ideal, remember that deep, sandy soil tires a horse's legs more easily, and the more tired the tendons, the greater the chance of damage. Conversely, hard ground is like a hammer hitting the leg, jarring it with every contact.

3. Dehydration. Take into account both the temperature and the humidity. If you have a ninety-degree temperature and the humidity is at ninety percent, you're going to have a problem. Generally speaking, if you add the temperature and the humidity together and your total figure is less than 130, heat stress should not be a problem. With a total figure of 150 or higher, especially if the humidity figure is forty percent or more of the total, the horse is going to have a tough time keeping himself cool while he's working.

If the horse is sweating profusely and really lathered, you'll know he's working hard You cannot keep him at that level of performance for very long. Give him a chance to breathe every few minutes, or more frequently if he needs it.

Remember, a horse can dehydrate without sweating a whole lot. The horse should not sweat heavily for over twenty minutes. If you have any thought at all that your horse is getting too tired to work safely, then back off. You don't want to hurt your horse. These are intended as general guidelines, so when in doubt, consult your veterinarian.

When working your horse in the round pen, never let another person take over from you, no matter how tired you may be. When you rest, your horse rests. If you let someone else work the horse, you won't be able to judge the animal's condition. Your horse won't have time to rest, and he may be in danger of heat exhaustion. Remember, if you are too tired to continue, the horse probably is too.

There is no specific rule on how long you can safely work. While you may get through a solid hour, you cannot work your horse that length of time without a break for fear of endangering his lungs. You have to give him time to breathe. Never hurt your horse in the round pen.

MOTIVATING THE HORSE

We'll need to motivate the horse to get him to change his attitude. The stronger the motivation, the quicker the change will happen. Also, the more natural the motivation, the easier and longer lasting the response will be. While it would be nice if we could use only food, or praise, to get the horse to do what we want him to do in all situations, it's just not likely. Removing the horse's fear of us is often not enough of a reason either. Although these motivations can, and do, play an important part in our training program, they won't give us the total results that we need.

What we're after is a change in the horse's thought patterns that will cause a change in his behavior. Motivation prompts change. To motivate the horse to change, we'll use his lungs and muscles. As the horse trots, he's using his muscles. Those muscles will work even harder at the canter.

At first, the horse is running from us. He's thinking, "How on earth can I get out of here?" Then he finds out that we're particular about the direction he runs. As he continues the process of running and moving, his tired lungs start calling up to his brain to figure out some options other than turning and running from us, to give them some relief. His lungs are yelling to his brain, "Honey! Help me out. I'm dying down here." This gives the horse a reason, or motivation, to change what he's doing, because what he has been doing isn't working to relieve his lungs, or his legs, or his muscles.

Now his brain starts looking for other options. Can he get out of this if he changes directions? Can he stop? Can he go over, or under, the fence? Can he kick or show aggression toward this fiend who is running him?

He has an unlimited number of options, not just two, and it's important that we realize this in all of our training programs. We tend to think that if we pull on the right rein, that the horse can only turn right. In fact, he has many options. He can rear up, lie down, back up, go forward, fall down, turn in any direction, and on and on. Turning right is not his only alternative. In training sessions in the round pen, it's no different.

Running the horse around the pen begins the process of the horse's learning what it is that we want from him. He will soon learn that if he looks at us, he doesn't have to move, or work. Thus, he relieves his pain. As he looks at us, his lungs will yell to his brain, "Atta boy, brain, we got it!"

The way we're using his lungs is to get him out of breath. Our intent here is never to permanently hurt the horse, so we must use caution and restraint when we're working the horse in the round pen.

When the horse's lungs ache, he will begin to change his attitude. Notice I said when the lungs ache, not when the horse is tired. If all we do is tire the horse, then the motivation is not strong enough to become permanent, and the lesson will need to be repeated day after day, in which case the horse only ends up in better physical condition.

Don't misread this. Hurt comes in all different levels, and what we are talking about is far less painful than what most training procedures call for. The pain we are talking about is the same kind we have when we run and get out of breath. But that type of pain is all that it takes to give the horse enough reason (or motivation) to change his behavior and his attitude toward us. Once that happens, the learning becomes easier for both of us.

If the horse is comfortable moving at ten miles per hour around the round pen, we want to push him up to fifteen. It's important that we're controlling the horse's speed and that the horse understands that.

Throughout this process we're actually controlling a large animal without ever touching him, and both the horse and the trainer begin to realize this. It's because of this learning process that the horse turns over more and more control to us and places us higher in his pecking order. So just as he would pay attention to a horse that's higher in the pecking order in the pasture, he will also pay attention and listen to us.

These lessons become more ingrained because the horse has gone through the learning process in a step-by-step manner. The lesson becomes permanent because the horse figured it out for himself, and having figured it out for himself, he will remember it longer.

CONTROLLING THE HORSE'S MOVEMENT

Now we'll set a goal. Our goal will be: to *control the horse's movement.* We will ask him for specific movements and will not let him wander aimlessly around the pen.

It's important that we not skip steps in any phase of our training, but this is especially true when working on movement control in the round pen. We will take the horse through a step-by-step program that will teach him that we are in control. This is the most important lesson of our training program.

We will start out with something as simple as possible: *to control the direction the horse is moving in.* The actual direction, whether left or right, is not important here. We'll use left as an illustration, but you can pick your own direction. What is important is that the horse goes in the direction you want him to, for this establishes a sense of your control in the horse's mind.

The horse has chosen to run, but we have chosen the direction in which he will run. He is running out of fear at first, and he thinks he's in control because he is running from us. The horse at this point can have his attention split. Perhaps his nose is pointing to the outside of the round pen. We'll let him run in that direction about four times around the pen before *we* chose to change his direction.

To change the horse's direction in the round pen, step toward the opposite side of the pen, away from the horse. As the horse comes around, come directly to the horse, almost to the fence. This presents the horse with a few choices: he can run over you, he can stand and face you, or he can turn around and run in the other direction.

If it looks as though the horse is serious about running over you, step aside and let him go by. When he comes around again, rather than confront you he will change direction. Eventually the communication between the two of you will improve, and the response time will get better. The horse's timing will get better from the moment you ask him to turn to the time he responds.

If the horse cuts back across the pen, circle around behind him and have him continue on to the right at that point, giving him time to make his turn.

Changing a horse's direction is also helpful if the horse is hyper and flying around the pen. By stopping and turning him, you are giving him a chance to breathe.

The next segment-goal will be to *have the horse switch directions* again. We'll assume that the horse is now running to the right. Again, we'll let him go around four times before asking him to switch, using the same technique we did the first time. If on the third time around the horse starts to change directions on his own and go back to the left, then, as quickly as we possibly can, we want to make him change directions and go back to the right for at least three to four times before asking again for our change.

The horse is now starting to realize that he is not only running away from us, but that we are chasing him. This is similar to bear hunting. You're hunting the bear and something happens and the tables are turned as the bear chases you. This changes things in a hurry. The horse is now saying, "Hey! This turkey's chasing me!"

On his third trip around, he's saying, "I understand that I am running from you, and that you are chasing me. Can I run any direction I want?"

If the horse changes direction on his own, quickly have him change back to the direction you requested. By doing so, you are now saying, "Wait, I didn't ask you to do that. I'll tell you when to change direction."

By responding to his question you are saying, "No, I want you to run to the right." Thus, the dialogue begins.

It's important to give the horse time to figure out what we want him to do. There is a big difference between making the horse do what we want, and letting him learn it himself.

We'll continue this process of having the horse turn back and forth, from right to left, until we can have him turn consistently when we ask. Remember, the object is not to chase the horse, but to control his movement.

Now we'll add a new segment-goal. We'll become more specific with our request. This time, we're going to ask him to *change directions at a particular post.* We're going to mentally pick out a post in the round pen and see how close we can get his nose to that post as he changes directions.

We will change his direction in the same manner as we did the first time, only now we are picking out a specific point at which we will have him change.

If the horse turns early, this tells us that we asked too early. If the horse maneuvers his turn twenty feet beyond the post, this tells us that we asked too late. By picking out a specific point, you find out how well you and the horse are communicating.

To correct your timing, you may have to move closer to, or farther from the post as you ask the horse to turn.

When we've got the horse changing directions at the post consistently, we'll graduate to asking him to not only change directions at the post but to *turn in toward us.* If you are asking the horse for an inside turn, do not walk toward the post. The closer you are to the post, the less room the horse will have in which to make his inside turn. By moving away from the post, you will give the horse ample room in which to make his turn to the inside. (Conversely, if you want the horse to turn to the outside, moving in a direct line to the post will give him less room to turn

to the inside, therefore encouraging him to turn to the outside.)

Say we've picked out the post where our horse is going to
change directions and face us, but instead he turns to the outside.
When this happens, as fast as we possibly can, we'll make him
change directions and return him running back in his original
direction.

This continues the dialogue. The horse is asking, "Is this what
you want me to do?" By your actions, you are replying, "No."

As soon as he goes back to the left, let him go around two times,
pick out a post and try again. Repeat the process, trying to stop
him as quickly as possible if he makes the wrong turn. Catch him
as quickly as you can and send him back in the direction he was
moving before you made your request. The quicker you can
change him, the quicker you are responding to him. When you
become more specific, the horse will understand what you want
him to do. The better we communicate with the horse, the more
he'll understand.

On his first mistake, after you let him turn to the right on the
outside (instead of making the inside turn you requested), you let
the horse go all the way around the pen one full time before you
stopped him at the post. On the second wrong turn he makes, you
let him go halfway around before stopping him. Continue stopping him at the half-circle point if he continues turning to the
outside. Keep asking for the change of direction, with the turn to
the inside. Within a few minutes, the horse will finally turn in
toward you.

Again, our segment-goal is for the horse to *turn to the inside
and reverse direction,* continuing to the right. As soon as he
changes directions to the inside, back up and give him room to
make his turn before letting him continue on to the right.

Be sure you practice this equally in both directions. You don't
need to perfect one side first, but it's easier that way. The more
consistently we can get the horse to turn toward us, the more
control we will have. Be sure the horse knows this lesson well, for
we're working with a graduated program and each step is integral
to the whole.

At this point we have the horse turning right, turning left, turning in to us, and we still haven't touched him. He's still not halter broken, yet we have gained quite a bit of control over him.

Our next segment-goal will be to *get the horse to stop moving his feet.* We need to understand that it is harder for the horse to change directions than it is for him to continue moving forward. When the horse changes directions, what he has to do at some point is to stop going in one direction and start going in the opposite direction. The stop the horse makes to accomplish this change may be only momentary, for a split second, but at least at this point we have a stop. So all we have to do is to improve on what we now have. We have a stop for one second. Now we'll get him to pause for two seconds, then three, and so on.

The more we have the horse change directions, the more apt he is to pause longer. Whenever the horse changes directions or stops, back off from him and leave him alone, no matter what direction he's facing. In this way he's learning that it's OK to stop. Remember, we're not interested in tiring out the horse, we're only interested in having control over him.

Now we're getting a conditioned response, which is the core of our training program. Once we're getting the pause consistently, we'll build on it by getting the horse to hold the stop longer and longer.

Our next segment-goal after getting the horse to stop, will be to get him to stop with his head inside of and facing away from fence. As long as he is running with his nose pointed toward the outside of the pen, he'll be thinking about leaving. When his nose is directed inward, or straight ahead, he's paying attention to the trainer. Obviously, if he isn't hanging his head over the fence, you won't need to worry as much about this step.

Again, one of our major training rules is that we must have movement. When we ask the horse to face inward, what we're asking him to do is to move his head and neck. In this case, to get that movement, we'll use a loud kissing sound. This sound will be used only to request movement. If we kiss to the horse and he doesn't move his head, then we'll have to do whatever it takes to have him move somewhere, or move some part of his body. We may have to slap our legs, wave our arms, or do anything else we can think of that will be an annoyance to the horse.

With this irritation, the horse might take off. If he starts to move off, make him hustle, telling him in effect, "At least leave at a trot, turkey." We'll then stop him again, as quickly as we can, and set up the same situation. We'll let him go a quarter of the way around the pen. If we can't, at first, get him to move just his head, then we may have to settle for his moving his entire body before we reset the same condition.

Repeat the process until you can get him to move just his head to face inside the round pen rather than outside the round pen. Each time the horse faces in or puts his head inside the round-pen fence, take a step backward and *be quiet.* Just stand still. You can also use a verbal cue such as "Good boy" or "Good for you." Again, you are communicating with your horse. By your actions and your voice, you are telling him he is doing what you asked him to do.

When we can get the response that we want, we try to improve on it. Again, the way we improve on it is to get the response for longer and longer periods of time. Each time the horse faces, or sticks his head outside, the round pen, we give him a signal (like the kissing sound), to bring his head and his attention back on this side of the rail.

Once we've got the horse stopped inside the round pen with his head inside the fence, we'll move on to the next step.

This segment-goal will be to *have the horse stand still and look at us.*

In order to achieve this, we want to make it as easy as possible for the horse. Once he's standing with his nose inside the round-pen fence, we'll move toward the front of the horse, staying ten to twenty feet away from him, whichever distance the horse seems to feel more comfortable with. Then we'll build on this, having the horse look at us for longer and longer periods of time. Just how much time we spend here will depend on the horse. The important thing in this lesson is that when we ask the horse to face us, he does.

Sometimes, after learning this lesson, the horse will think that he is always supposed to stop and face us. If we want him to leave, and he wants to face us, we should use the beginning lesson outlined in this chapter (asking the horse to move) to make him leave. It's important that the horse respond to our requests instead of doing what he wants to do.

TOUCHING THE HORSE

Our next segment-goal will be to *approach the horse and rub his head.*

How close you can get to the horse varies with each animal. Obviously, if you're dealing with a hand-raised, halter-broken horse, you will be able to be closer to him in a much shorter period of time than if you are dealing with a three-year-old ranch colt that has never been handled. With a green colt, you may only be able to get within thirty feet of him before he gets scared and runs off.

It's important to keep in mind our objective here, which is not to run the horse, but to *not* run him. If we can get within twenty feet of him with him standing there, not moving, then that s where we'll begin.

During this lesson we will not carry anything in our hands that might appear to be threatening. We will not raise our hands toward the horse as though we were going to feed him, or pet him, as these actions may make him feel uncomfortable, or even threatened.

At this point the horse does not understand what we are asking of him. If we begin walking toward him and he leaves, or begins to run, then he is left with a lingering doubt in his mind as to what our intentions are. However, if we can get him to stand still twenty feet from us, and then *we* turn and walk away, the horse will no doubt be surprised at our movements and will be thinking, "Oh, is that all he wanted? Just to get that close to me."

We are now at the place in our training where we're getting the response that we want and we will begin to improve on that response by repeating this condition. We'll approach to within twenty feet, stop, turn and walk away. When we can consistently get to twenty feet without the horse's leaving, then we will move a step or two closer, say to eighteen or nineteen feet, before turning and walking away.

Again, if the horse moves off at this closer range it is because there is some lingering doubt in his mind as to our intentions. We'll give him the opportunity to stop by himself and turn and face us. We can then move back to our original distance and begin to repeat our sequence of stopping, turning and walking away until he seems less wary. At this point we can again try stepping up to nineteen feet.

If at any point we feel that the horse is about to run or leave, it is far better for us to walk away from him than to continue to approach until he does leave. In this way we will be raising his level of apprehension (by approaching him) and then lowering it (by turning away). This nonthreatening gesture will result in a change in his attitude as he begins to think, "Gee, I'd like to learn what is expected of me."

We'll proceed with our training by slowly and gradually shortening the distance between us and the horse until we are standing one to two feet away and directly in front of him. If, at this close proximity, the horse begins to move his head to look away, we'll step in the opposite direction, while making the kissing signal. This asks the horse to bring his head, and his attention, back to us.

Once I feel comfortable that the horse will not move off, I raise my hand to rub him. I will reach up and touch him between his eyes, not on his nose, because the nose is more sensitive, and if I touch him there, he will be more apt to jerk back and move away. The horse will be more cautious about his nose and mouth than he will be about the space between his eyes. I'll touch him here for a second or two, before turning and walking away, letting him know that's all I wanted. Repeat this step several times.

Remember the petting rules we talked about in Chapter One. No hard pats or slaps, and no tickling. A good firm rub or stroke is best.

It's important not to chase the horse's head with your hand if he moves. If you do, he will take his head farther and farther away from you, eventually taking his feet too, and you'll be chasing the horse around the pen again.

At this stage in your training, always make the horse look at you with both eyes.

Now we can rub the horse between his eyes consistently. As we stand here and rub his head, he is learning that the longer he stands here, the less he has to work by running. This is strong motivation for the horse to stand by us.

Being able to pet the horse has another advantage. We can use petting as a sign of approval. In all areas of our training, we can improve the horse's learning time by telling him when he gets things right, rather than letting him guess. A stroke or rub will tell him we are pleased and that he has responded correctly to our request.

Verbal cues are also good. Some people don't like to talk to their horses, some do. If you feel like talking to your horse, that's great. The horse will adapt to your language, and to mine. Also, I haven't used the word "whoa" in the round pen yet, because I can't control the horse. I can't make him stop, I can only give him the opportunity.

THE STRONGEST HALTER ON EARTH

Our final segment-goal for this stage of our training will be to get the *horse's attention riveted on us, no matter where we move or stand.*

We'll follow the same procedure as when the horse was looking over the fence.

We've been petting the horse, so we are a few steps in front of his head. Whenever the horse drops his head down to the ground or begins to look away from us, we'll give him the kissing signal to get his attention back on us. This way he learns that as long as his head is in the right position, he doesn't have to work and that we will stop harassing him.

Once we have the horse continually looking at us, we'll begin moving away from him and closer to the center of the round pen. The horse will be standing by the fence, continuing to look at us.

If, as we move, he drops his head or looks away, we'll ask (kiss) for him to bring his head and neck (and attention) back to us. Eventually we should be able to stand ten to fifteen feet away from the horse, toward his hip, and have him bend his neck around and look at us for longer and longer periods of time.

As we stand off from the horse's shoulder at a distance of ten to fifteen feet, the horse's neck will begin to tire and he will square up his shoulders to match his neck. When he does this, he will be moving his feet, turning and facing us. It's not necessary to control a thousand-pound horse, we just need to control one part of his body. If we get the horse's nose within two feet of the gate, the odds are pretty good that the rest of him will not be far behind.

The lessons the horse has learned in this chapter will make him more pleasant to be around. We've taught him to always turn and face us when we ask, so when we walk into a stall or pasture, the horse will not turn his tail to us and run. This is a beginning step in teaching him to be caught. It gives us a way to control the horse

The strongest halter on earth is the horse's mind.

so we do not have to approach him and catch him by walking by his rear end. This lesson is also the foundation of teaching the horse to ground-tie, to stand still while being saddled, to spook in place, and to understand that we're in control at all times. It develops his attention span, and teaches him not to ignore us when we walk into a pasture or stall. While the round pen is helpful, it will not solve all the problems we'll face after we've started to ride.

We'll use this technique of asking the horse to face us in getting our horse over such fears as having his feet picked up, being clipped, and being given a bath.

The horse doesn't run really well backward. If we're having problems picking up his feet, and the horse starts to move away from us, we've taught him to recognize a specific cue (the kiss), which asks him to turn and face us and to stay there. We've developed, or are in the process of developing, the strongest halter and halter rope possible, which is the horse's mind.

STEPS TO GAINING CONTROL

We'll now review the eight steps you need to reach in gaining control of the horse:

1. You can get the horse to move.
2. You can control the direction the horse is moving in.
3. The horse changes direction upon your request.
4. The horse stops and stands still when asked.
5. The horse turns his head in your direction.
6. The horse looks at you for longer and longer periods of time.
7. The horse allows you to approach him and touch his head.
8. The horse's attention is riveted upon you, no matter where you move or stand.

Chapter Three

Halter Breaking and Leading

R emembering that horses, like people, vary in learning speeds, we can apply the following lessons over several sessions, or over several days. Speed is not important.

TEACHING THE YOUNG HORSE TO LEAD

If you are working with a young foal, one that has not yet been weaned, take him into the round pen. Keep the mare outside but tied to the pen. This way, as the young foal moves around, he will stay within a few lengths of his mother and will not be running the entire distance around the pen. If the mare does not tie, remove her from the pen and place her elsewhere.

The young horse should be comfortable with being handled. He should be used to being rubbed and petted all over.

When working with our horses, we will not use chains over the nose, under the chin or anywhere around the horse as they will only cause additional problems for both of us.

Many of the steps we utilized in gaining control of the horse's movement (see page 43) must be mastered before we put a halter on a colt and begin the leading lesson.

If you are working with a horse that has not been handled much, it is very important that you take him through Chapter Five, "Sacking Out," which will add two more crucial steps that are necessary *before* you begin to halter break him. These are:

1. You should be able to rub the horse's entire body.

2. The horse should allow himself to be touched and rubbed all over with a rope.

Only after the horse is thoroughly comfortable with these steps is he ready to progress to being halter broken.

We'll begin by sending the colt once or twice around the round pen. When working a young horse, don't let him make more than three trips around the pen without letting him stop and rest. It's important not to overstress young horses, as their legs and lungs are fragile. How hard you work them should be dependent upon their age and condition, as well as the weather. Again, if it is very humid or hot, you will not be able to work the horse as long.

Ask the colt to look at you. Don't let him run continuously around the pen, instead, turn him back and forth on a small section of the fence.

When putting the halter on the horse for the first time, don't hurry or grab him. It's more important that the colt be relaxed when we do put the halter on, than where it is actually placed. This may mean that the halter will be hanging at an angle, perhaps dangling over one ear and hanging down in front of his face. If we work slowly and with care as we adjust the halter to fit correctly, the colt will accept it without fear or resistance.

Once the colt has accepted the halter, we will teach him to lead. For this lesson we will keep the halter on him and add a burlap sack.

There are several reasons for using the sack. A rope placed around a horse's body can rub the hide off between his legs, and since we will be applying pressure (by pulling on the rope, which will be attached to the sack), we want the pressure to be spread out over a larger area of the horse's neck than if we used a lariat.

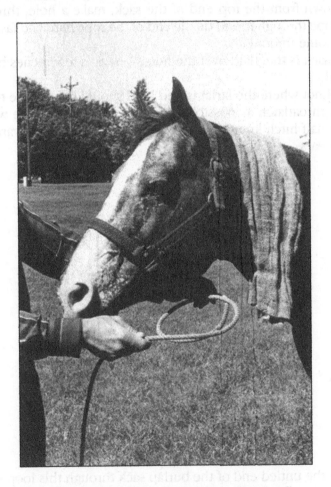

The sack is placed a few inches below the horse's poll.

Also, with some older horses, more pulling may be necessary, and if a halter or a lariat is used, the horse's poll may become tender and he could overreact to that soreness.

Any pain given a horse during his training, either through riding or ground work, actually slows the learning process by taking the horse's concentration off what he is supposed to be learning and on to the pain area. So the burlap sack lessens the pain and fear, resulting in quicker learning for the horse, and quicker results for us.

Take a burlap sack and fold it in thirds lengthwise. About one inch down from the top end of the sack, make a hole, thread a lariat rope through it, and tie the end of the rope hard and fast so it won't come undone.

The sack is then laid over the horse's neck, a few inches below his poll.

The knot where the lariat is tied hard should be as close to the horse's throatlatch as possible. I make a loop in the rope with a double half hitch knot, the top end of the loop going toward the horse's ears.

A double half hitch knot.

I pull the untied end of the burlap sack through this loop until the sack fits snugly around the horse's neck. I then tie another

The knot where the lariat is tied to the untied end of burlap sack should be close to the horse's throatlatch.

double half hitch knot around the sack, and this time pull the knot tight to keep the sack from tightening around the horse's neck.

When beginning this lesson with a colt that has never had a rope, or any other kind of restraint on him, we only want him to accept the feel of the pressure, and so we won't yet ask him to actually turn and face us.

Standing to one side of the colt, near the middle of his body and at a distance of about eight feet, we will begin this series of exercises by putting a slight pressure on the rope to encourage the horse to bend his neck in the direction of the pull. When working with the horse on this lesson be sure to reward him often when he gives in to the pressure you are applying. His reward comes when you give him slack in the lead rope. At first, he may not be actually turning in to you, so you may be rewarding a look, or a lean in your direction.

When he responds correctly, we will let him straighten out his neck before we reapply new turning pressure. As he becomes consistent in his response to the rope's pressure, we'll increase the pull to get him to bend his neck even farther. When we reach this point, the horse will begin to move his feet and turn to face us. As he does so, he releases the pressure on his neck.

It is important that we move to the other side of the horse and repeat the lesson so he is accustomed to giving in to pressure from both sides.

Be sure to release his head when his neck is bent in your direction. If he begins to straighten his neck, promptly take the slack out of the rope, before he gets his head completely forward.

Our next segment-goal will be to get the horse to follow the pull of the rope, rather than being pulled by the rope. We'll begin with a slack rope. If the colt begins to move away from us, we'll gently pick up the rope and let him walk into some light pressure. He'll feel the pressure and stop.

The longer rope gives us more time to gradually add pressure to the burlap sack. Likewise, if the colt begins to run, a short lead rope would not give us time to react slowly and gently. With a foal, it's tempting to manhandle him and show him who's boss. However, in doing so, a percentage of colts will get hurt. Take some time and treat that baby as though he could drag you off.

The following exercises will outline the progressive steps in teaching a colt to lead and will improve any horse's leading.

We'll teach the colt to lead by asking him to move from side to side, not forward. This means that we will be applying pressure from each side of the horse. We will stand on his left side applying pressure until he gives in, then we will move to his right side, repeating the pressure until he bends. The forward motion will come after he learns to give in to the pressure he is feeling, instead of pulling against it and fighting it.

Halter Breaking and Leading

Again, it is important to always reward the youngster for any lean of his body toward us, even if he does not actually turn in to us. Release the tension on the rope, pet and praise him.

We will continue with this exercise until the colt begins turning his body and begins to follow us when we put slight pressure on the rope. At first he may only move a few steps. Since we are standing off to one side of the horse, as he takes more and more steps, and as we keep turning to exert pressure on the rope, we will actually be making a circle. As the horse moves a step or two, keep only the slightest pressure on the rope. Remember, we want to always use the *least* amount of pressure that it takes to get the response we are seeking. Keep asking for a few more steps, enlarging the circle until the horse is moving forward with you.

When the colt is finally moving forward, move behind him and ask him to move forward in front of you. As he does, give him a little slack with the rope at first, and then add pressure with the rope until he responds and turns toward you. Remember to release the pressure as soon as the horse begins to turn. Gradually ask him to move away from you a little faster. This exercise will help teach him to respond to the pressure, and not resist when he feels the pull on his neck.

To discourage dragging and hanging back, drive the horse at a considerable distance (say ten to fifteen feet) in front of you. Since the horse has been through the round-pen lessons, he knows to move off when you ask him to do so. The distance will be reduced as he understands that he must keep up his pace in order to stay in front of you as you drive him.

In order to get the horse to lead closer to your shoulder, where he should eventually be, stand at his shoulder and begin walking toward his nose, turning in tight circles around to the right and then in tight circles around to the left, making the horse walk around you.

The steps to this point are:

1. The horse is comfortable wearing a halter.
2. The horse is comfortable wearing the burlap sack around his neck.
3. The horse has accepted the feel of pressure on the rope.

4. The horse responds and turns toward us when he feels pressure on the rope.
5. The horse begins to follow us when he feels slight pressure on the rope.
6. The horse moves ahead of us when asked.
7. The horse begins to lead close to our shoulder.

Now we're ready to thread the rope through the halter. The burlap sack will stay on the horse's neck, and the rope will come down between the horse's lower jaw and the lower part of the noseband of the halter.

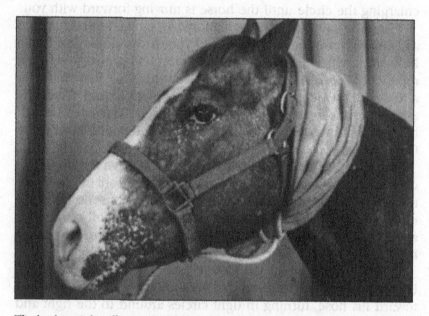

The burlap sack will stay on the horse's neck and the rope will come down between the horse's jaw and the lower part of the halter's noseband.

Turn the colt in tight circles to the right, and to the left, so he becomes familiar with the pressure of the halter on his nose. When these steps are accomplished at the walk, then progress to the trot. As before, let the colt work out in front at first. Then gradually bring him back to trotting a little closer to you.

Finally it's time for just the halter and the lead rope, so remove the burlap sack. Practice the same exercises explained above. This is an excellent beginning on the leading lesson.

From untouched to trotting alongside us can be accomplished in less than two hours, but as training times may vary with different horses, remember that the lesson can be spread over several sessions or days, to fit the horse's pace of learning.

TEACHING THE OLDER HORSE TO LEAD

Sometimes we encounter older horses who may have had exposure to people, but who have had very little handling, and no haltering or leading lessons.

We will begin by taking the horse through the steps outlined in Chapter Two and at the beginning of this chapter. We will then progress to placing the halter on the horse and will advance to putting the burlap sack on him. If the horse doesn't want us to put a halter on him, that's OK. Instead, we can work on his turning right, turning left, and facing in toward us rather than hanging his head over the fence. Eventually the horse will say, "Gee whiz, I wish he'd just let me stand still and put the halter on me."

Once the older horse accepts the halter, we will use the same steps we did on the colt. We will stand to one side, and apply pressure to the rope, immediatly releasing it as he follows us with his head, then with his body.

Many times the older horse will refuse to move forward, and will begin to pull back on the halter as he feels pressure. The violence of his reaction will depend upon how trapped the horse may feel.

We do not want to play the game of who can outpull whom, as this would be a major mistake and would actually teach the horse to refuse, in addition to teaching him to pull back when tied.

We must keep in mind the exercises we are going through are like building blocks. Each one is important to the next. If we inadvertently teach the horse to pull back at any stage, that error will show up later on in the training. Often, the roots of a horse's problems can be traced to poor foundation training.

Whenever leading any horse that pulls back or balks, immediately change what you are doing so you get his feet moving. Then get his feet to move every time. After that, get the horse's feet to move in the direction you want them to go. Keep that movement. Don't let the horse stall out on you.

If the horse refuses to move forward, turn him in small circles.

Just as all people do not react the same way in similar situations, all horses do not respond the same way either. While one horse may walk away after we have the rope on him, making it easy to introduce the pressure of the rope, another may refuse to move at all.

Our initial round-pen training teaches the horse to turn and face the trainer. After he has learned this, it may be more difficult to move the older horse far enough away, for a long enough period of time, in order to teach him to bend his neck and to give in to the pressure of the rope. Use noise, the lariat, or a longe whip, to insist that the horse move away from you. Do whatever it takes to get him to move out.

As the horse walks away, apply slight pressure on the rope. Once he feels the pressure, he may even take a few short bucks. If this happens, he will probably stop fairly quickly and turn and face you. Why? Because he has already learned that he is going to be all right if he does so.

If we let the horse stop and stand at this point, it will become even harder to get him to move away from us the next time. Keep him moving without applying pressure on the rope. Remember, he needs to move so he can be taught to respond.

If a horse refuses to move with a rope on, then take it off and retrain the horse on moving, turning, and moving away when asked. What we are doing is: (1) Returning to that segment of our training program where we *can* get the response that we want. In this case it would be to get the horse to move on command without the halter, (2) getting the response consistently, and then, (3) building on the response. As applied here, the improvement that we are seeking is to get the horse to move off with the halter and rope on. Once we are successful at this stage, we are ready for the next step, which is to get him to move off to the end of the rope and stop. At that point we add a little pressure to the rope and have him bend his neck toward us.

We can improve the quickness of the horse's response by

getting him to move away at a faster gait. If he pulls too hard, we'll return to a slower gait.

Next we'll ask the horse to walk in front of us. He may fight the pressure of the rope and begin to drag us. As he continues around the pen, note how he softens his neck and stops throwing his head. Even the pull will lessen as he arches his neck toward us. With practice, the horse will become even more relaxed and accustomed to the pressure of the rope, and will give in to its pull.

Leading is nothing more than giving in to the halter. All of our exercises should be designed so the horse is bending his neck and giving in to that pull.

A more advanced lesson is to place the rope over the horse's neck from the other side, so that when you pull he will be forced to turn his head and body away from you, following the direction of the pull of the rope. This is more difficult for the horse because he has become accustomed to following the lead and turning in your direction.

Begin by pulling from the same side of the horse the rope is on and then walk past the horse's rear end and pull. As the horse begins to turn better, it will not be necessary to cross over to the side the rope is on, because he will be turning in the direction of the pull of the rope, following you.

When we are through practicing all the exercises, the horse should lead with very little effort. The more these exercises are practiced, the better the horse will lead.

PULLING BACK

Most of us at one time or another have come in contact with a horse who pulls back. Even one who has been pulling back for years can learn to accept standing tied. We need to teach this lesson in a way that the horse understands, and in a way where neither the horse nor the trainer will get hurt.

Defining what the problem really is will help us when we begin to teach the horse that we do not want him to uproot posts, trees, hitching posts, or us.

When a horse is pulling back while standing tied, he is fighting and resisting the pressure and pull of the halter. It doesn't matter whether that pressure is coming from our pulling the horse forward, or whether it's from the horse pulling back from the post, it still feels the same to the horse.

Our goal is to get the horse to stand calmly when tied. It doesn't make sense to tie our resisting horse to a post or other solid object, because then we would be starting our lesson with our goal. Approaching the lesson in this manner would mean that we would soon need bigger and stronger halters and ropes, and what we would be doing is reinforcing the horse's resistance. We need to teach the horse not to resist whenever he feels the pull on the back of the halter on his neck. He needs to learn to give in to that pressure.

Before we begin this lesson we should have taken the horse through all of the exercises for teaching the older horse to lead. Even if he leads beautifully, if he is ever unmanageable or pulls back when tied, take him through the lessons. Concentrate on initial round-pen work. Then, when you have the halter and lead rope on him, practice making the horse move off, having him turn toward you, then being driven in front of you; and lastly, practice putting the rope over his back and having him turn. When practicing these lessons, the horse should wait for us to put pressure on the rope before he turns and faces us. Make sure he relaxes his neck before he moves his feet to turn and face you. As we go through these lessons, in essence the horse is standing tied to us, and we are a moveable post. We will use the same burlap-sack-and-rope method that we used in teaching the young horse to lead.

Next add a little speed to the exercise when, as the horse moves away, you ask him to turn toward you. Gentle pressure should be all that's needed to get the horse to bend and relax his neck when he makes a turn, even at a trot.

When you pull on the rope, move in behind the horse so the pull comes from more directly behind him and will feel stronger to him. This will give you a better advantage to get a quicker and more abrupt stop. This abrupt stop will prepare the horse for what he will feel when pulling away from a post.

As the horse makes his turn he will cock his head toward the pull of the rope, indicating he is ready for the turn. This is good because he is also anticipating stopping. When he is tied to the post, we will also want him to stop moving.

The next exercise is to put the rope over the opposite side of the horse's neck and have the horse follow the rope, the way we did in the leading lesson. Again, the horse will be asked to do this turning and stopping exercise at increasing speeds. If the horse stops but does not soften his neck toward the pull of the rope, keep some pressure on the rope until he relaxes his neck and turns. Don't worry about having enough strength, a five-pound pull works just as well as, if not better than, a hundred-pound pull. It just works slower. Don't give up.

The horse that pulls back is excited. That usually means he gathers steam, or speed. We purposely excite him during these exercises so that we may, in turn, ask him to relax, bend his neck, stop pulling, and stop his feet. As we practice these lessons, the horse is thinking about stopping, and we are thinking about making him move. When we get to the post, the horse will still be thinking about stopping, which is what we want him to be thinking about.

When the horse will bend his neck at the slightest pressure of the rope, then we are ready to move him to the fence. We will simulate his being tied there by looping the rope around the fence post, as in the diagram.

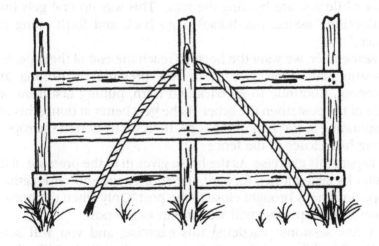

Simulate the horse's being tied by looping the lariat once around the fence post.

Do not tie the rope or wrap it around the fence post in any way in which it could snag and tighten. It is important that the rope be free to slide around the fence post easily.

A really strong fence is not necessary, however it is important that it will not cut or injure the horse if he brushes up against it. Do not use barbed, or any other type of wire fencing.

At first, leave some slack in the rope so that the horse can move ten to fifteen feet from the post. Ask him to walk off a little. As he does so, gradually add pressure to the rope until he turns and faces the fence.

If the horse did not turn, but instead began to pull back on the rope, let go of the rope and return to the previous lessons of having the horse give in to the pressure of the rope, without using the fence. Only when he is doing this well should you return to looping the rope around the fence post.

If the horse turns and faces the fence, then move to his other side. This will entail flipping the rope over the horse's head and body so that you are pulling on the opposite side of the post. If the horse becomes tangled in the rope, or scared, drop the rope and start over again.

If the horse pulls back at any time, drop the rope, walk toward him, pick up the rope on the other side of the post as the rope comes through. Keep your hands at least five feet away from the post while you are holding the rope. This way no one gets hurt.

Continue asking the horse to go back and forth along the fence.

Remember, we want the horse to reach the end of the rope, feel pressure, and then give in to that pressure by turning and stopping. Continue to go back and forth, pulling first from one side of the post, then the other. As he gets better at doing this and responding to the pull of the rope, then we'll shorten the rope to bring him closer to the fence.

Repeat this exercise. As the horse gives in to the pressure of the halter by taking a step forward, use shorter and shorter lengths of rope until he is brought close to the post. Only when the horse is comfortable up close will we tie him to the post.

A few sessions practicing this exercise, and you will see a noticeable difference in your horse's standing tied and leading.

ADVANCED LEADING

Advanced leading lessons will improve any horse's leading skills. It's absolutely necessary to master all previous leading lessons before beginning these final exercises. These lessons are especially helpful in handling stallions safely, before, during, and after breeding season. Problem stallions with long histories of poor manners can be corrected and trained using these exercises.

In teaching this lesson, it is important to be specific.

Our goals are:

1. The horse's nose should be even with your right shoulder.
2. When you stop, the horse should stop and back up two steps.
3. When you back up, the horse should back up.
4. When you step toward the horse's right front leg, he should pivot on his hindquarters.
5. When you turn around to the left, the horse should move around you, without bumping you.
6. If you turn and face the horse and ask him to move his hindquarters, he should move over.

If we teach the horse to never run in front of us, then the chances are good he will not run and drag us off. We need to understand that when the horse is leading, he is giving way. When he walks forward, his rear end pushes his front. When he backs, his front end begins pushing his rear end.

It is easier to teach the horse to give way backward than it is to teach him to come forward, so that's where I begin.

If I take the halter and yank on it, the horse's head will go up as he reacts to the pull. If I pull hard enough, his front feet will start to go up, and then he will rear.

So to teach the advanced leading lesson, a buggy whip will be used to hit the horse below the knees. The whip will get the horse's attention, yet does not hurt the horse if used with restraint. You can put protective gear on the horse's legs if you like. When we threaten the horse's front legs, his head will go down.

When backing the horse, do not hit him above the knees. As a general rule, three hits or less, then stop, pet the horse, and let him think about it. That's a lesson I learned from my horse Dream. I could hit him three times. More than that, and he thought it was abuse.

The noise of the whip hitting the ground may be all you need to get a response. Do not be too quick to criticize or correct the horse. Accept little improvements and reward the horse often by petting him.

Our first goal is to teach the horse to keep his nose even with the trainer's shoulder—the ideal placement of the horse in relation to the trainer when the horse is being led.

We visualize that we are starting at the base of a triangle, and we will progress through specific steps to work the horse up the triangle.

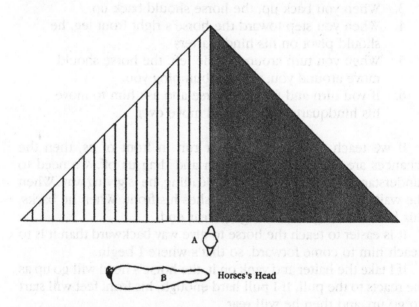

Progressing through specific steps, we will work the horse (B) up the triangle until he is within a six-inch area, even with our shoulder (A).

We'll start out by not expecting too much. We will not correct the horse as long as he is in the shaded area. Gradually as he becomes more consistent, the area we will accept will change and will get smaller until the horse's nose (B) is even with our shoulder (A). (See diagram.)

We will mentally divide the triangle in half, represented here by the solid and shaded areas. The horse is not to cross into the black area. When his nose is in the black area, ahead of the trainer, he will be corrected. Whenever the horse is in the white area, outside of the triangle, he is generally too far away to correct. So we'll stop, get him back in the shaded area, and start again.

To begin, use the fence in teaching the horse to move back. Placing the lead in your left hand, ask the horse to back just a few steps, then stop and pet him. If you ask the horse to move back and he does not, then start with hitting your leg, or the ground, with the whip, which is held in the right hand. If he still does not back, then hit him on his legs below the knees. If you decide you need to hit the horse below the knees, give him a good whack, don't dink with it. If he jumps out in front of you, stay with him and keep the whip on his legs until he stops, and then have him back a few steps.

Continue in this manner until he learns to move back consistently. Always keep slack in the lead rope.

At this point do little or no forward leading, only backing. When the horse learns to consistently stay behind your shoulder, then it's time to start training on how to move forward, while staying even with your shoulder.

The cue will be your shoulder movement, not the pull of the lead. You don't want to drag the horse around. Your shoulders signal your movement, then you start to walk. If you teach the horse to move with your foot movement, he is always going to be a step or two behind. He shouldn't drag on the lead. If you decide that it will take five pounds of pressure to move the horse, then that's what it will take.

Shorten the lead rope, placing your hand within four to five inches of the halter ring. This will keep the horse close enough to control, and will put him in a good range for you to be able to tap him high on his hip. If his nose comes too close to you, take the butt end of the whip and drive the nose away from you. Allow the horse to move ahead of you without reprimanding him. He can move anywhere in the shaded area of the triangle during this phase of training. However, do not let the horse turn a complete circle. If the horse continues to circle, let him know that he has gone too far by hitting him below the knees.

Once the horse learns not to hang back and begins to move forward in response to your motion, consistently reduce the shaded area. Each time the horse becomes consistent working within the boundaries of that area, advance him by reducing the distance he can move both forward and back. When the horse will move forward and stop, take two steps back, and stay next to your shoulder, he is ready for you to add another exercise.

Step toward the horse's nose in a tight circle to the right. Have the horse step back a little, pivot on his right rear leg, and move away from you.

This exercise will help if the horse is leading too close, or leading at an angle with his head in and his rump out. If the horse does not step away, just use the handle end of the whip to tap on the lower part of his nose, or on his neck, to keep him moving away.

As the horse becomes more aware of the trainer, he will have less of a tendency to step on, or spook into, him. Combine these three exercises as one practice unit until the horse understands. As he becomes more consistent, you can practice the exercises at the trot.

The next exercise is to get the horse to turn around us, without bumping us. He is to soften and bend his body, stay close to the trainer, and when finished with the turn, stop and back up two steps.

Take the halter and lead rope off the horse in the round pen, and practice all the exercises again. When practicing, be specific with your requests.

Now take your horse to a larger arena and, once more, practice all of the movements. When finished here, you will have exceptional control over your horse. If you have done a good job, when you lean forward without moving your feet, the horse will lean forward without moving his.

One step further in developing an advanced leading horse is to train him to take a small jump. With the lead in hand, stand to one side of the jump and have the horse jump toward you. Do this only after completing all previous exercises. This exercise will help in teaching the horse to land away from you when jumping or stepping over something.

Most horses, regardless of breed, can jump small jumps comfortably. Many can jump larger ones as well. These exercises are not only good leading practice, but can be fun for both you and your horse.

Chapter Four————————

Facing Fear

I t's unreasonable to ask a horse not to be afraid. That's like my telling you to go into a bad area of town for a walk at two in the morning, and not be frightened.

While we can't ask a horse not to be afraid, we can teach him how to handle his fear. Any horse can be trained to overcome his fears. This lesson can be taught even to yearlings.

Our goal will be to teach the horse to turn and face the object he fears. He will then calm down, and we will be safer on him than if he had panicked, turned, and run.

If you haven't put your horse through this training and you are riding in a forest and you hear a motorcycle coming but you can't see it, turn your horse to face the direction of the noise. You know you're already in a wreck, you just have to decide how bad it's going to be. But you sure don't want that motorcycle behind you where the horse can't see it. It's like that old saying, the things we can imagine are always worse than reality. The same is true for your horse.

While I can't control the horse's fear, I want him to be afraid with all four of his feet on the ground. Anyone can ride a frightened horse that has all of his hooves firmly planted on Mother Earth.

Also, we can't possibly show the horse everything in the world there is that might frighten him. We need a way to get him to calm down from his excitement *before* we get into a wreck.

I had a man come up to me at one of the symposia.

"John," he said, "My horse is perfect during the Western Pleasure classes. He does everything just great, except for one thing."

"What's that?" I asked.

"Well, when I take him back into the ring to pick up his ribbon, he goes crazy when the crowd breaks into applause. How can I stop this?"

Hmmm. I suggested he could do one of two things. Either he could hire two hundred people to sit around and clap until the horse got accustomed to the noise. Or he could teach the horse to control his fear. He chose the latter.

Horses shy at all sorts of things. Watching a dressage show not long ago, I noticed a handsome bay. He could do the pattern beautifully, but he was afraid of the umbrella shading the judge's stand. If that horse had been put through the exercises in this lesson, he still might have been afraid of the umbrella, but he would have passed it by as though it weren't there.

Once our horses are trained in controlling their fear, we won't have to blame the umbrella, the baby stroller, the barking dog, or the floating balloon for our horse's coming unglued. Because he won't.

Last year some people came to me with a show Arabian. Again, this was a horse that knew what was expected of him in the show ring. Physically and mentally he could go out and do his Western Pleasure class to perfection. Emotionally he was a time bomb. If a plastic sack fluttered in the ring, he'd run over anyone in his flight path.

We placed the horse in the round pen and brought in a large plastic tarp. The owners were pretty worried, because they just knew there was going to be a major problem. I started working the horse on crossing the plastic. Within ten minutes, I was riding him on a loose rein with his head down, across the tarp. He had learned to control his fear, and as a result, he was a much safer horse to ride.

Teaching a horse to spook in place is a harder lesson for him than teaching him to just stand in place, because his fear makes him more emotional.

To get our horse to face his fears, we'll begin in the round pen. If you don't have a round pen, you can use a square pen, or a square arena. When you use something other than a round pen, the arena size has to be such that the horse can't run to an area and stop and wait for you to get there. You must be able to control the horse's direction at all times.

The disadvantage of using a square pen is that the horse is going to run into the corners and get hung up there. He will also challenge the fence more in a square area than in a round pen, for that option looks better to him.

If you're working in a square pen, you must teach the horse to stay out of the corners. He'll run up there and get stuck and feel that his only avenue of escape is over the fence. If this happens, move behind the horse and get him to move again. He'll run to the next corner of the pen and do the same thing. Again, move in behind him and get him moving. He'll go to the next corner. Repeat. Until he learns that the corners aren't escape routes, he'll keep trying them. Remember it's both more dangerous and more difficult working a horse in a square pen.

The horse will be running free, without a halter. Am I in more danger connected to him or standing thirty feet away? Am I in more danger tying him to a snubbing post or letting him run free?

Am I in more danger on the ground or on his back? I am at least fifty percent safer on the ground than on his back for this lesson. If you do this lesson before climbing on the horse for the first time, it will make you much safer on that first ride.

Before beginning the lesson, make sure that your horse understands how to turn in to you when you ask. It's very important that he knows that part of the round-pen lesson well before beginning this training. He should also turn in equally well from both sides, right and left.

Now we're in the round pen, the horse is here without a halter, and we're going to play a game with him. My part of the game is to scare the horse and make him run. The horse's part is to stay there and face me.

There is one rule to the game. I can't hit the horse. The most I can do is to flick a rope at him, if I choose to use one, touching him lightly on the top of his back. If I touch him at all, the horse should move. He doesn't need to be hit. What do we do when someone slaps us hard on the back? If the horse has any pain whatsoever, he would not stand there. Neither would you.

We'll scare him a little bit at first. We'll use something that will be the least threatening thing to the horse and the simplest thing of which the horse can overcome his fear. If you start with a six-foot piece of plastic, you might run him through the fence. You might have to start with a chewing gum wrapper, then build your way up to the plastic.

Starting slowly, we'll make a raspberry sound. When doing so, always make the horse turn and face you. If he dashes away from you to the left, be sure that he comes back to you from the left. If he chooses to escape, then he must travel the same route on his return trip.

If we make a frightening sound and the horse stands still, we'll go up to him and pet and praise him. Keep repeating the raspberry sound, then praising him each time he stands calm.

If the horse takes a few steps, which indicates that he's thinking about leaving, but doesn't move, again praise him. He's beginning to control his fear.

If the horse gets into the habit of leaving, then move him around the round pen for two or three minutes to give him time to think about it. Be careful to make sure that the horse doesn't misinterpret your actions and think that running around the pen is what you want him to do. You can help prevent miscommunication by stopping him every turn or half turn and giving him more opportunity to stop and turn in and face you.

As he's running around the pen, he's probably getting tired and the old lungs are once again saying to the brain, "Can't you think of something better to do?" As soon as the horse stops on his own, quit scaring him. The horse will soon grasp that when he stops running the scary thing goes away.

Be attuned to your horse during this lesson. If you turn around and walk away and the horse runs, he probably thinks that's what you want him to do.

We'll continue playing this game as we add a little more pressure. We may move from the raspberry sound on to a loud grunt, then to a shout, and then a shout combined with wildly waving our arms. We can work up to almost anything, and eventually, no matter what we do, the horse will stand and not run off.

I carry my rope into the round pen with me because the horse has seen it during earlier round-pen lessons and he should be fairly comfortable with it. I'll now flick the rope at him. Each time the rope touches the horse and he hesitates but doesn't run off, I'll go up to him and praise him.

I've chased horses with practically everything, including chain saws and banging barbecue lids. I don't expect the horse to get accustomed to all of the noise and commotion, my goal is to teach him to control his fear. Whatever is used to create a sense of fear, once the horse is no longer afraid of it, go on to something else.

Again, while it's impossible to expose a horse to all the fearful things he may encounter, we can teach him to face fears, and by doing so, we will end up with a calmer, safer horse to ride.

Chapter Five

Sacking Out

T he old-time cowboy used a grain sack to get a horse used to being handled. By rubbing and gently slapping the horse, he would "sack him out" to get him accustomed to being touched. Today this is still an important lesson for the horse, for it gets him used to the feel of our hands, ropes, and saddle blankets, and teaches him that he can trust us when we're working around him.

Before we begin to sack the horse out, it's important that we have not only read Chapter Two, but that we have taught the round-pen lessons to our horse. The sacking-out lesson will be a logical continuation of rubbing the horse's head. Our goal for this lesson will be to *have the horse relax with a saddle blanket on his back.*

TOUCHING THE HORSE

Since this lesson should begin with the least aggressive approach to the horse, we will begin using our hand to sack him out. At the end of the round-pen lesson, we were petting the horse on the head. Now we'll build on that.

Our first segment-goal will be *to be able to rub the horse all over his body with our hands.* Again, we can further break down this goal into smaller segments, such as touching him first on both sides of the neck, then both shoulders, both front legs, and so forth.

Once we feel that the horse is comfortable with our being in front of him rubbing his head, then we begin to rub his neck and side and back with our hands. Talk to him during this process. "Good boy. That's it."

It is important to turn and walk away from him frequently. Then reapproach and return to rubbing him.

The horse should be trained at this point to stand still whenever we approach. The act of approaching by now should be the cue that will trigger the conditioned-response to stand. If, during this lesson, we stand here petting him the whole time, then we're not setting up the cue very often. So when we come in with the saddle blanket, if we've only approached him once, we're going to have more trouble than if we'd come up to him twenty times during this lesson.

Walking away also erases the question mark in the horse's mind as to what we're going to do with him.

Again, if you feel the horse is going to move off at any time, your retreat before he jumps or moves away will erase the question in his mind. He'll think, "Oh, that's all he wants. Well, that's better than running around this dumb pen."

The more questions you erase in his mind, the more confidence the horse gains both in himself and in you. We raise his fear level a little by approaching him, then we turn and walk away. The horse is learning to control his fear. Eventually he'll learn that if he stands still, we will finally leave him alone.

When we get to the point where we pet him for five or ten minutes, we're building his confidence and his trust of us.

We will continue in this manner, rubbing the horse all over his body, with the exception of his ears and nose. We'll cover these areas in a minute.

We will use a progressive approach in touching the horse. In order for a horse to accept our picking up his legs, we need to first be able to touch his shoulder. Touch the shoulder and walk away. Then progress down his leg in the same manner, touch and walk away. If you think he's becoming nervous and is about to kick, stop.

Remember, the goal is not to have the horse move, run off, or kick us, so it's important to do things that won't get him so upset that he thinks he'll have to fight back.

Your movements should be natural. Don't be too quick or too hesitant in your actions. If you have a doubt that you can touch the horse's hip, then you need to spend more time at his belly. If the horse sucks up his stomach, or draws back from your touch at any time, take care of the problem by rubbing the area again and getting him to relax.

Proceed slowly, moving over his entire body, including his mane and tail, and under his belly.

Be sure to pet the horse equally on both sides. Reaching over the horse and rubbing the off side while you're standing on the near, will accustom him to the saddle blanket flopping over his back. Be aware as you do this, that the horse may jump to get away from your hand, and in so doing, may run over you.

Also by petting one side of the neck and then the other, and by alternating shoulders, and so on, you reduce your chances of startling the horse when you get on the other side of him. If you work only one side at a time your horse will have the tendency to always offer you that side, avoiding placing you on the side that has not been worked.

THE HORSE'S EARS

Handling the horse's ears is an important step in our training for several reasons. When we climb up to ride the horse, if we have not taken care of any fear he may have of our touching his ears, and we reach down to pet him while we're on his back, he may get scared and begin bucking, because he is head shy. We will also need to put the headstall over his ears when bridling. If the horse is throwing his head at that point, we may cause further problems by bumping his teeth with the bit.

It's dangerous for us to be standing by a head-shy horse, because the swinging head can knock us down, or even break our nose.

In getting the horse used to having his ears handled, we will start again with rubbing his head between his eyes. We'll take our hand briskly over his ears, proceeding down his neck. Once we can achieve this without the horse moving his head, then we'll begin to slow our hand down. As the horse becomes more comfortable with our hand touching his ears, we can leave our hand on them for longer and longer periods of time.

If the horse begins moving his head away from your hand, do not grab onto his ears or head, or try to force him to stand there. Also, never try to force your horse, with your hands, to stay with you.

Repeat the process, speeding up a little bit, to the point that you can get your hand over his ears and to his neck, without his moving his head.

We will use this system for any head-shy or ear-shy horse.

PRELIMINARY BIT ACCEPTANCE

Now we'll move on to the horse's nose. In touching this area, at this point it will be good to rub the horse's nose all over with our hand. Start at the eyes and come down, rubbing all over the horse's face.

We'll get the horse used to accepting the bit by using our hands. We'll take our fingers and insert them into the side of the horse's mouth and touch his tongue. It is not necessary to squeeze the horse's gums or put pressure on his tongue to have him open his mouth. If you lay your index finger on the horse's tongue, he will try to spit your finger out by opening his mouth. You can also rub the horse's lip on the outside and run your finger under his lips to the upper part of his gums above his front teeth. This will help because you'll be touching these areas when you are placing the bit in his mouth.

Put your right arm between the horse's ears with your hand coming down between the horse's eyes and resting on his forehead. Your elbow will stay at the poll as you rub the horse between the eyes. When you put the bridle on your horse, your hands will be in this position, so it will be easier to teach him now to accept this movement, and this touch, than when you have a cumbersome headstall in your hand.

If your horse has a tendency to raise his head up, or the horse is much taller than you are, you can teach him a specific cue to drop his head. Place your hand between the horse's ears and exert extremely light downward pressure on his poll. As the horse begins to raise his head up, increase the pressure slightly. As soon as he begins any downward motion, immediately release the pressure, to the point where you take your hand a half inch off his head. Repeat this process until the horse has learned the cue that every time you put your hands on the top of his head, he will drop his head. Teaching this cue should take fifteen to thirty minutes.

Once the horse responds consistently to your hand by lowering his head, you can graduate to using your forearm, laying it between his ears as you did before, and then pretend you're putting the bridle on the horse. Use the left hand as though it is holding the bit. Take your left index finger to lift up the top of the horse's lip and place your thumb on top of the horse's tongue until he opens his mouth. When he opens his mouth, take your hands down and pet the horse.

If the horse refuses to open his mouth, reach in the side of his mouth toward the back of the gap between his front and back teeth, with all four of your fingers, and rub his tongue really well. He'll open his mouth now, because he has a gob of digits in there. Whenever he opens his mouth, you'll take your fingers out and pet him, letting him know that's what you want him to do.

From the initial contact on an unbroken, unhaltered horse, the rubbing process can take anywhere from thirty minutes to three hours. We have now achieved the following goals:

1. We can rub the horse all over his body with our hands.

2. The horse is comfortable with our hands moving over his ears.

3. We can rub the horse all over his nose and head.

4. The horse drops his head when he feels light downward pressure on his poll.

5. The horse opens his mouth when we pretend to put in his bit.

HORSE FOLLOWS YOU

Our next segment-goal will be to *get the horse to follow us around the round pen*. This will be important because if we can have him follow us to the middle of the pen, we'll be safer there as we approach him with a lariat, saddle blanket, and saddle. We will be in little danger of getting squashed against the fence should the horse become nervous. Working in the middle of the pen will give us plenty of room to get out of the horse's way should he buck or jump.

As we're working on the horse with our hands and rubbing him all over, he is learning that while he's standing by us he does not have to work. Since the horse is basically a lazy animal, this is his preference. We can use this to our advantage in teaching him to come to us and to stay with us when we begin to walk away from him.

Before we can get the horse to stay with us, he has to move his feet. While rubbing the horse, we'll step out two to three feet from his side and ask him (by making the kissing sound) to look at us. The horse will turn and look at us as he's been taught to do in the round-pen lesson. Remember, he can look at us without moving his feet.

As his neck tires, he'll move his feet around to square up his shoulders. We'll repeat this process several times, moving farther and farther toward the horse's rear end, encouraging him to turn a greater and greater distance to stay with us.

Once we can move directly behind the horse and ask him to turn and face us, and he obeys, we're ready for the next step.

Standing to the side of the horse's head, two to three feet away, we will walk toward his head, causing him to move his head away from us. Eventually he'll also move his feet. The reason he is going to move his head is to avoid our walking into it.

Now the horse is executing a turn away from us. Facing the same direction as the horse, we'll continue walking with him as we make a small circle to the right. His throatlatch will be about even with our shoulder. As he stays with us, we will gradually begin to move in a straight line.

If the horse stops moving, or slows down, then we'll immediately walk back toward his head and ask him to take a few steps off toward the right, again navigating a turn.

Eventually the horse will stay with us in a straight line. If he walks away from us, we will give him the kissing signal. Since he has learned the meaning of this, he will turn and face us. We'll position ourselves and the horse correctly and begin again.

Moving into the horse and causing him to make a circle will also work for snubbing horses or halter training. Remember, we need movement in order to train.

Be sure to settle for less in this procedure. Once the horse begins to stay with you, you don't need to insist on his taking a great number of steps before praising him. If he stays with you for a step or two, stop and praise him.

Extend the time you spend walking with the horse until he follows you around the pen.

THE LARIAT SACKING

Our next segment-goal will be to *rub the horse all over his body with the lariat.* It's a sure bet that if the horse is afraid of the lariat, he'll be afraid of the saddle. We'll use a soft lariat rope, the same medium-lay calf-roping rope we discussed in Chapter Two. Do not use a heeling, or an extremely stiff or hard, rope. Whips are too threatening to the horse. You could also use a dish towel, a soft cotton or nylon halter, or a soft cotton lead rope, if you prefer. For the purposes of discussion here, we'll use the lariat, however the steps would be exactly the same for any of the substitutes.

We'll begin this phase of sacking out the horse in the same manner that we approached the horse the first time in the round pen. Coiling the rope will make it smaller and less threatening to him.

We can begin by touching the horse's neck with the rope. Remember, our objective is to touch him without his leaving or moving off. If we touch the rope against the horse's neck and we feel that he will move off in three seconds, we'll take the rope away in two, then walk away.

If the horse starts moving his feet, I'll sometimes stay with him if I think I can. I don't want to take the rope away because that tells him how he can get out of his situation. I'll give him the opportunity of not having to run. Sometimes this doesn't work and the horse moves off. If this happens, move him around the pen a couple of times before again giving him the opportunity to stop.

We will continue this process of approaching the horse, rubbing him with the rope, and then walking away. Rub the horse with the rope all over his body, his legs, and then his nose and ears. Continue working with the lariat, on both sides of the horse, until he is very comfortable, to the point of being bored.

By rubbing the horse's legs with the rope, you're establishing a basis for handling his feet, which we'll cover in Chapter Nine.

Once you can consistently rub the horse with the rope all over his body without his moving, then begin with light bounces of the rope, until you can lightly bounce the rope all over the horse's body as he remains standing still.

The above segment-goal should take fifteen to thirty minutes to reach. Once this is done, move on to the next step.

THE SADDLE BLANKET

I use Navajo-type blankets, made of soft wool or cotton, for saddle cloths on my horses. These are not the real thing, handwoven by the Navajo Indians, but rather that type of blanket. I like them as they let air get to the horse's back.

The purpose of a pad is to make an ill-fitting saddle fit your horse. By using Navajo blankets, I can add more blankets if I need more padding. To avoid bulk, I stagger them from side to side (near side long, off side short, then near side short, off side long) so I don't have a big lump under my leg. You want your saddle to comfortably fit your horse with the least amount of padding so you can have close contact with him.

The most important thing about a saddle blanket is that it be clean. A clean blanket feels better to the horse and will prevent a lot of chafing and discomfort to him. Folding a Navajo blanket in half gives you four clean surfaces to each blanket, which allows for a number of saddlings before the blanket has to be washed.

Sometimes I'm asked about orthopedic pads. I personally don't like them as I find they are hot for the horse.

Now that's out of the way, we'll move on to our next segment-goal: *putting the saddle blanket on the horse's back.*

Like all of our training, we can break this into smaller steps, or goals. We'll actually be repeating the process used to accustom the horse to the feel of our hands and, later, the lariat.

Begin in the middle of the round pen with one saddle blanket. Fold it into about a twelve-inch square. (You can also use a dish or bath towel at this point and change to a saddle blanket later.)

Approach the horse with the folded blanket. Let him smell it, taking your time until he is through examining it. Rub his nose with the blanket. Proceed to rub the horse along his head, ears, neck, shoulders, back, and legs. Again, work on both sides of the horse.

If the horse leaves, hurry him off. In this way, there's some punishment for not controlling his fear. The next time, he'll reconsider standing and controlling himself. Have the horse run one to two trips around the round pen before giving him the opportunity to stop. Remember to be attuned to your horse, for there is the danger that he'll get the impression that you want him to run. If you feel that he does think you want him to run, stop him and turn him more often.

Any time the horse runs or moves away from you, he is telling you, "I'm not comfortable with what you are doing. Keep working until I relax." This is a good dialogue, for it keeps both the horse and us from being hurt.

Once he stops, back up a step with the saddle blanket, fold it smaller than it was before he took off, and begin again.

Once you can walk up to the horse with the blanket folded up, with the horse relaxed, then begin rubbing the folded blanket all over his body, belly, and legs on both sides.

Now unfold the blanket, making it twice as large, and reapproach the horse. Every time you unfold the blanket during this lesson, do so *away* from the horse.

Proceed as you did with the twelve-inch folded blanket. As the horse becomes comfortable with each rubbing, gradually increase the size of the blanket until it is completely open and you can approach the horse, holding one top corner of the open blanket in each hand.

Place the blanket over the horse's ears and over his neck. Throw the blanket onto his back from either side.

Leave the blanket on the horse and put hand pressure under his belly where the cinch will go, to get him used to this feeling. Be sure to reach down and touch the inside of his legs, because you'll be doing that when you saddle the horse and you don't want that to be the first time you touch him there.

Pat the blanket with your hands. Adjust it. Move it up and down the horse's back. Take it off. Put it back on. Repeat until the horse is completely relaxed with the process. By doing all of this, you won't have to spend time with each additional saddle blanket. Get him very comfortable here before moving on to the first saddling.

Sacking Out

Place the blanket over the horse's ears and neck.

PHOTO: UNA SEELEY

Pat, adjust, and move the blanket until the horse is comfortable with the process.

PHOTO: UNA SEELEY

Chapter Six

The First Saddling

I t is possible for you to do the round-pen lesson, sacking out, saddling, and first riding in a matter of a couple of hours. But before you approach the saddling lesson, be sure you have not skipped any of the lessons outlined in Chapter Two.

Since you can't tell if a horse will buck on that first ride, waiting thirty days won't help. It's better to saddle and ride the horse now, because everything is still new to him. He's been running around the round pen, and that's new, the saddle blanket is new, and now we're going to be putting a saddle on his back, and he'll say, "OK, what's new?" If we wait thirty days, his response is likely to be, "Oh no, what is *this?*"

Before we can ride the horse, he needs to be comfortable with a saddle on his back. The horse doesn't need to be halter broken. You're actually safer not being attached to the horse for this lesson. Remember, any time we try to confine or restrict the movement of a reluctant, thousand-pound animal, which has phenomenal power, we're looking at a potential wreck. It's important that the horse doesn't feel trapped when we are saddling him for the first time, so even if he is halter broken, we will not have anything on his head.

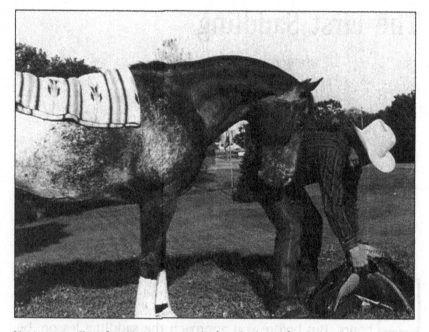

You're actually safer not being attached to the horse for this lesson.

I can put a saddle on almost any horse with a halter and a lead rope in ten minutes. That's not my goal. It's not important to merely get the saddle on, it is important that we get the horse to relax when he feels it on his back.

Our goal for this part of the lesson will be *to have the horse stand calmly while he is being saddled.* This will also teach the horse to stand quietly, without physical restraint, while he is being groomed and while his feet are being handled. I don't mind spending three hours or thirty hours on this lesson as long as, in the end, the horse understands what I want.

There are two reasons a horse resists the saddle. One is attitude, the other is fear. If I spend the time to train him correctly the first time he's saddled, then I know the second saddling will be fine.

You will be working with the horse alone. Never have someone else work with you on this, because the chances are good that the horse will hurt one of you.

First, check the horse's attitude. Is he listening? If not, he may have to go around the pen a time or two in order for you to get his attention.

It's important to start this lesson in the middle of the round pen, where you have already placed the saddle and blankets. This central position will reduce the chances of the horse getting the saddle hung up on the fence. You will also be safer here, for you'll have room to get away if the horse jumps or bucks.

Since the horse has by now been taught to walk with you when asked, walk him to the center of the pen.

Begin the lesson by coiling the rope and rubbing it over his body. Bounce the rope on and off his back. He should be accustomed to this from the earlier sacking-out lesson.

Next approach the horse with the folded saddle blanket and rub him with it. Unfold the blanket and bounce it off the horse from both sides. Now fold the blanket in half and place it on his back in the proper position for saddling. The horse is now ready for the introduction of the saddle.

I usually saddle for the first time from the off, or right, side, of the horse. Saddling from the right side is easier because I only need to throw over the latigo from that side. From the near, or left, side, the cinch, back cinch, and breast collar would all have to go over the horse.

Put up the opposite (left-side) stirrup. Now, as gently as you possibly can, set the saddle on the horse's back. It is important that you are gentle, and that the opposite stirrup doesn't come crashing down into the horse's legs, for this will not only frighten him, but could send him running over you in order to get away from his pain.

*Saddling from the off side is easier since only the latigo
must be thrown over the horse's back.*

If you are going to be riding with a flank cinch and breast collar,
attach these items on your saddle before putting it on the horse.
The flank, or back cinch, keeps the pressure off a horse's withers
when you are roping calves. It also helps keep the saddle from
being turned when roping a reluctant animal. If you are riding
with a flank cinch, make sure that your flank cinch connector, the
piece of leather connecting the front and back cinches, is secure.

The First Saddling

If it is not and it happens to come undone, your flank cinch will quickly become a bucking strap as it slides farther back on the horse. Also make sure that the connecting strap is not too long, for it's possible for a horse to get a leg hung up in it.

The breast collar helps the saddle stay forward when you are in rough country and climbing hills. As you place the collar on the horse, be sure that it rides a little above the shoulder so you are not inhibiting the animal's movement.

If the rear cinch and breast collar are too large for the horse, remove them.

Again, it's *all* new to the horse, so he won't be in a panic, thinking, "Oh, what is this new thing the turkey's putting across my chest now?"

Now, walk around to the opposite side and immediately take the stirrup down. This will eliminate the chance of its slipping off the saddle horn and scaring the horse.

Make sure that your cinches are straight and the saddle strings are pulled out from under the saddle.

I'm frequently asked what kind of a cinch I use on my horses. I don't like fleece cinches, so I use a combination cotton and nylon cinch. Like the saddle blankets, the important thing is not what you use, but that it is always clean.

When you are ready to reach for the cinch, be sure to keep your legs ahead of, but not blocking, the horse's front legs. This way, if the horse jumps forward, or kicks, you will be out of the way of both his front and hind feet.

Reach under the horse for the latigo, keeping your hand well to the front of the horse, behind his front legs. This puts you in the safest position possible for this part of the lesson.

When securing the latigo, take a couple of loose wraps before tightening it up. We will be securing the saddle with a latigo knot, rather than the eyelets, for this first saddling. By using the latigo wraps, the saddle will be less likely to loosen and move under his belly if the horse moves off before we are ready. Also, if he moves off, we may be able to hold on to the latigo and talk him out of leaving.

Gradually tighten up the girth. Make it just as tight as if you were going to ride. Again, we do not want the saddle slipping under the horse when we move him off. If he bucks, he'll quickly learn that he can't buck the saddle off, and better he learn this lesson without either you or me on his back. Check your flank cinch, if you are using one, to insure that it isn't too long. Again, a horse can hang a leg up in a long flank cinch. And he doesn't have to be scared to do it; just kicking at flies is sometimes all it takes.

The horse should stand still for all of this because he has learned to trust us in the preceding lessons. He should never take a step. If he does, then we know that we didn't do as good a job as we should have up to this point.

If the horse moves off when we approach him with the saddle, then we didn't do enough with the blankets; if he moves off with the blankets, we didn't do enough with the rope, and so on back down the line.

Again, our goal is not to chase the horse around the pen, but to have him stand there calmly while we saddle him. If the horse makes a tiny mistake, maybe a step or two, don't punish him by making him run. Step to his side and ask him to turn to you and begin again.

After the horse is saddled, we're in a dangerous position. His first step with this thing on his back is apt to be a big one. Since we've spent quite a bit of time teaching the horse to follow us, we don't want to turn our back on him and have that step include us. Back away from the horse and move him off. Be sure you do not take your horse for granted, whether he is a mustang or a backyard pet. Even the gentlest of horses may buck or kick at the saddle the first time. In so doing, he may hurt you.

It's a normal reaction for a horse to buck with a saddle on his back, so expect it and get out of his way. This does not mean that he will buck with us on his back. The reverse is unfortunately also true. If he doesn't buck with the saddle on his back, it doesn't mean that he won't buck with us up there. Also, we don't want to assume that just because a horse has been saddled once, he won't buck on the second saddling or with a different saddle on his back.

Let the horse run around the pen as he learns he cannot throw the saddle off. This gets him accustomed not only to the saddle, but to the fenders and stirrups slapping against his sides. Do not worry if the horse goes down with the saddle on his back. Many times he will not roll all the way over. If he does, and if you have a good saddle, your tree should be fine. This is an escape attempt by the horse, and he will soon learn that rolling with the saddle will not release him from it.

When the horse calms down and seems comfortable with the saddle, return to him.

STEPS TO SADDLING

We'll now review the steps to saddling. They are:

1. Have the horse's attention.
2. Approach the horse and rub him with the rope. Rub the horse under the belly and on the legs with the rope. Bounce the rope on the horse's back and on his off side.
3. Approach with a folded saddle blanket and rub it on the horse. Approach with an unfolded saddle blanket and rub and bounce it on the horse from both sides.
4. Place the folded saddle blanket on the horse's back.
5. Set the saddle gently on the horse's back.
6. Tighten the cinch.
7. Back away and move the horse around the round pen.

Now, play with the saddle. Pull on the horn, lift the cantle up and flop it against the horse's back, pull on the saddle strings, move the stirrups back and forth, lift and drop the rear skirts, and lift the fenders and snap them against the horse's sides.

If the horse runs off, let him run halfway around the pen before giving him the opportunity to stop. When he does stop, begin again.

The purpose of all this crashing around with the saddle is to get the horse used to the commotion, to the sounds and the feel of the saddle leather against his body. It is far better to have this happen when we are not on his back or connected to him in any way, so if there is a wreck, we do not have to be a part of it.

Once the horse is comfortable with your banging the saddle and fenders around, it's time to snub him up to another horse.

SNUBBING UP

Snubbing up a green horse gets him used to something above his head (our body), which is where we will be when we ride him. This lesson should be done in the round pen by someone who

Snubbing up a green horse should be done only by someone who's had a great deal of experience.

has a good deal of experience with horses and who also has an experienced snubbing horse. If you do not have these qualifications, I strongly recommend that you find a seasoned horseman, with a seasoned horse, to help you with this task. If you don't have a snubbing horse, or someone to help you, just go through the next step very slowly. There have been millions of horses that have been broken without a snubbing horse.

Any time you put two horses in close proximity to one another and add the ingredient of a rope, you are looking at a situation loaded with danger for all involved—horses and rider.

If you are snubbing a mare in season to a stallion, you are further increasing your chances of having an interesting, and probably unpleasant, experience.

You do not want to wrap the lead rope around the snubbing horse's saddle horn unless you have a lot of experience working with horses. All you need is to have your hands loose. If the green horse gets away from you, he can't go too far in the round pen. If, at any time, you feel that you are getting into a predicament with the green horse, just let him go. You can always go over and get him back. That's not a problem, replacing a finger can be.

Ride the snubbing horse up close to the saddled green horse. You will only have a few feet between where the rope connects to the horse's halter, or neck if you are not using a halter, and the snubbing horse you are riding.

If you are wearing spurs, be sure they are short shanked; you may get a long-shanked spur hung up in the green horse's saddle fender, stirrup, or flank cinch.

Begin by moving the two horses around the pen. If the green horse will not readily follow, use the same system you used in getting him to follow you around the pen. Turn the seasoned horse in to him, causing him to move his head away, and eventually his feet. Now you have movement, the first step in training. Walk with him.

As he relaxes and becomes accustomed to being connected to another horse, reach over and pet him along the neck. This reassures him and helps get him over his fear of having something (you) above his head. If all of our work has been on the ground and the first time he sees movement above his head is when we're on him, we could have a problem. So pet him from above.

Reach over and pet the horse to accustom him to having someone above him.

Tug on the horn of his saddle, pull the saddle strings, and bump him in the shoulders and along the saddle fender with the toe of your right boot. Bump him along his sides so he gets used to feeling bumps and won't overreact to them. Lift the back of the saddle and let it bounce on his back. The goal here is not to torture the horse, but to get him accustomed to the feelings and sounds that are likely when you are riding him.

Take a coiled lariat and slap it against his saddle. Rub it along his neck and ears and across his croup. This is important, for if you accidentally brush your leg against him while you are dismounting, you may be in for a big surprise.

Only when the horse is comfortable with all of this should you think about getting on his back. But there's one more step before we get to that.

THE FIRST BRIDLING

I use a full-cheek snaffle bit with my horses. This bit has no shank and doesn't need a curb chain, and that makes it easier to put in the horse's mouth the first time. Use an average size, broken (jointed) mouth piece, not too fat and not too thin. It is also very difficult, if not impossible, to pull a full-cheek snaffle through a horse's mouth.

Understanding the use of a D- or O-ring, or a full-cheek snaffle can lead you to a higher performance level with your horse. Specifically, the snaffle bit is designed to give us more direct control over the horse's head. With proper use of the snaffle, we can work that control throughout the rest of the horse's body.

Many people get discouraged with a snaffle because when they pull back, their horse doesn't stop as quick as they'd like, or maybe even not at all. They reason that if they put a bar bit, or even a more severe bit in the horse's mouth, he will surely stop. This type of thinking is not completely incorrect. In fact, in some instances, such as for horses to be ridden by children under fourteen, it may be the best answer for maintaining control.

However, if you are trying to improve the performance of your horse, or trying to reeducate a horse that is giving you control problems, then understanding what the snaffle bit can do will make your training of the horse much easier.

The snaffle is designed so that it makes it easy for you to get your horse's head to one side or the other. Why is this important? Every time your horse's ears are in line with his tail, you are building inflexibility in his body. Whether we call it inflexibility, or resistance, or heaviness, or clumsiness, or a general lack of responsiveness, this is not a quality we want in our horses, so we need to overcome it. Even if we feel resistance, if turning the horse feels like we are turning a Mack truck, or he's throwing his head, or he won't turn, or stop, or back, or he's charging forward, or not standing still, or he's running away with us—all of these problems can be solved with the snaffle.

Our final goal in our training, when we have reached our highest level of horsemanship with our horse, is when he can move forward with his ears in line with his tail in a completely relaxed manner, as though he is floating on air and waiting for our slightest cue. Again, this can all be achieved with nothing stronger than a full-cheek snaffle bit.

The full snaffle also spreads pressure better than the O-ring snaffle. With the O-ring snaffle, the off side spreads pressure and sores the horse. The D-ring snaffle spreads the pressure better than the O-ring, but again, you need a curb strap. You can also pull the bit through the horse's mouth.

I do not use a cavesson, because this impairs the horse's communication with me. If the horse opens his mouth, he's trying to say, "Let go of my mouth." If I clamp it shut with a cavesson, then I've cut off his means of communication.

The day we need the most control is the day we have the least. That day is the first day we ride the horse. If a snaffle bit is enough to ride him with today, it should be enough to ride him with tomorrow and for the rest of his life.

To say that a horse has a hard mouth is absurd. The toughest mouthed horse in the country will feel the lightest touch possible on his mouth. If he will feel your finger pressed lightly against his mouth, he will surely feel a forty-pound pull against the bit. The same horse will find the tiniest bit of grain in his feed bin. So if we have a "tough-mouthed" horse, we must realize that we need to reeducate his brain, not his mouth.

I use the snaffle over the bosal because I have found that I can put the snaffle on the horse on the first day without any problems. I really haven't found any good reason for using a bosal over a snaffle. The answer here is not the bit, but how we communicate with our hands to the horse.

As my communication improves, I'll get to the point where I can do anything with him in a snaffle. Then if I want to go to something lighter, I'll work him in a halter, then a neck rope, then nothing at all.

Riding without a bridle has a few advantages. When you go trail riding, you have one hand free for a Coke and one free for a sandwich. If you're as bad a roper as I am, this system also gives you two hands to try to rope with.

When people see Zip work without a bridle they sometimes say, "He's a superhorse." That's not the case at all. You can ride any horse without a bridle. We are talking about a system of control that will work with any horse.

But let's get back to the green horse we're getting ready to ride.

Since we worked with the horse's mouth in Chapter Five, it should not be a surprise to him when we repeat that lesson here. We'll fool with his lips and put our fingers on top of his tongue, pretending we are putting in the bit. Remember, we do not need to hurt the horse in any way to put a bit in his mouth.

Since we've taught him that every time we bring his head to the side, he is to drop it, we won't release his head unless he's relaxed.

Our right hand will put the bit in his mouth. Bringing our hand between his ears, we'll lift his lip with our left index finger. Be sure you look to see where your opening is. Put the bit in the horse's mouth. Switch hands with the headstall and smoothly flip his ears into it. Never bend the horse's ears.

Check for a proper fit for the bit. You can't tell by looking at the outside of the horse's mouth, so open it and look in. If the bit looks comfortable, not too tight or hanging down in his mouth, then it is probably right. Use your own judgement. If it seems to make the horse smile, loosen the headstall a notch or two. The exact placement is not all that critical, but in order for the horse to be comfortable, the bit should not be flopping down from the corners of his mouth. It needs to be right at the corners, but not pulling them back.

You never want to practice putting a bit in and out of a green horse's mouth. Put it in, leave it in, and when you're done riding, take it out. It is enough to get it in nicely the first time. With an older horse that has had problems in this area, we'll spend more time putting the bridle on and off.

Let the horse walk around the round pen, mouthing the bit and getting the feel of it in his mouth. Let him walk around with it in, for ten or twenty minutes. That's usually enough. He doesn't need to eat with it, sleep with it, or wear it for days.

The horse will chew on the bit for five to twenty minutes before stopping. Any chewing after that means we're doing something wrong. When he learns he can't spit the bit out, he'll quit trying.

As for reins, I use round reins with a knot in them. You may use whatever you are comfortable with. Be sure that they are not so long that the horse might accidentally step on them.

Once the horse is fairly comfortable with the bit and saddle, you're ready to ride him.

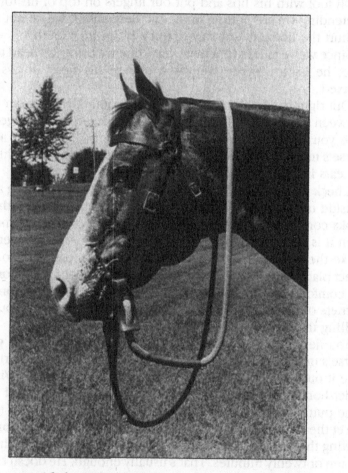

A good fit for the bit is right at, but not pulling back the corners of the horse's mouth.

Chapter Seven

The First Ride

*A*t this point we have worked with the horse quite a bit. He is comfortable with our working around him, he follows us when asked, he remains calm as he is saddled and bridled, and he is accustomed to seeing us above him. The saddle fenders and strings have been popped around him, and he is not overly concerned with movement of the saddle.

I am not interested in riding bucking horses. There are professional rodeo riders who do that. If I can't get the horse to accept the saddle and move around the pen comfortably, then how can I expect to get on his back and have him do what I want him to do? That's why, for this lesson, it is very important that we have done our homework by taking the horse through Chapter Two ("Round-Pen Reasoning"), Chapter Four ("Facing Fear"), Chapter Five ("Sacking Out"), and Chapter Six ("First Saddling") *before* we get on him for the first time. In this chapter, as in all of our lessons, we must always ask ourselves, am I asking too much of the horse? Is it too much to ask the horse to trot around the round pen without a halter? To carry a saddle? To carry me? If at any time I feel that I am being unreasonable, then I'll back off.

A lot of times in the symposia, people will tell me that their colt, who has never before been ridden, probably won't give me any problems. After riding over two thousand of these creatures, let me assure you that no one—even that person who has been with the colt since his birth and has worked with him every single day of his young life—can tell if a horse is going to buck, or not, when he is ridden for the first time.

People think that whether or not a horse will buck is influenced by the amount of weight that is on his back. I see a lot of macho guys who will put their wives and daughters on their horse for the first ride, reasoning that she's light, so the horse probably won't buck, "but if he does, I can hold him." This is fallacious thinking.

Let's take ten average horses. You can present this lesson the wrong way, and at least sixty percent of them will not buck at all when they are ridden for the first time. That leaves four. Of those four, on two of them you can do half everything wrong, and they won't buck. Now we have two horses left. Of those two, you have to do things at least eighty to ninety percent right for one of them not to buck. And that last little sucker? He still may buck. Regardless. You can do everything right and occasionally a horse will buck. That's just the law of averages.

While we can't keep that last horse from bucking, nor can we identify him, we can improve our odds by insuring that we do everything right with all ten horses.

Now, let's ride.

Pop the stirrups and pull the saddle strings just as we did for the first saddling (Chapter Six). Do this on both sides of the horse. Lift the cantle several times, and bounce the saddle on the horse's back. Once the horse is comfortable with this, we're ready to get on him.

As we get ready to take our first ride on our green horse, it is important that we be as relaxed as possible so that we don't transmit any nervousness or anxiety to the horse. Controlling our own fear is probably the most difficult part of this lesson.

While riding with spurs this first time will probably help teach you to keep your legs off the horse, you will be safer if you don't wear them for the first ride. Also, do not wear loose clothing or a loose belt that may get hung up over the saddle horn.

Take the reins and the horse's mane in your left hand, taking pressure off the withers. The slack should be out of the left rein, with the right rein loose. In this way the horse can still have his head forward. This means that we are not cheeking the horse, or pulling his head way around to the side. We are letting him look straight ahead in a relaxed manner, but if he jumps forward as we mount him, we can pull the left rein hard, pushing the horse's rear end away from us, thus reducing the danger of his kicking us. Remember, the reins don't mean squat. Right now, the horse has absolutely no idea what that bit in his mouth is supposed to do.

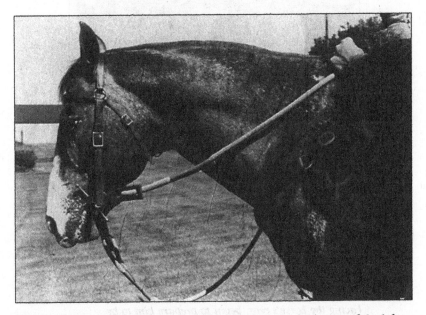

When mounting a horse for the first time, the slack should be out of the left rein, and the right rein should be loose.

The horse is standing still. He has accepted all of the things we have done to him up to this point.

Face the rear of the horse. The closer we stay to him, the less pressure there will be on him when we mount, and the less likely he will be to move away from us or walk off. Don't put pressure on the sides of the saddle, or on the saddle horn. Also, do not put your face in front of the horn.

Facing the horse's rear, begin to prepare him to be mounted.

The First Ride

As we put our left foot in the stirrup we need to be standing in front of the horse's front legs. If he starts to move off, we'll take our foot down, step back, ask the horse to come toward us, and pet him. We will repeat this step, of just putting our foot in the stirrup without placing weight on it.

When the horse is comfortable with this, we will begin to put weight on the stirrup. If the horse starts to move, we'll remove our foot, again pulling on the left rein to move the horse's head toward us and push his rear end away.

As the horse relaxes, we can begin to put our weight in the left stirrup and, moving our left hand from the mane to the horn, step up. We'll go halfway up, standing with our left foot in the stirrup, our right leg swinging free next to the left stirrup.

The reason we move our hand from the mane to the saddle horn is, that way, if the horse should buck, or move abruptly, our stomach is not over the horn. Our right hand will be on the cantle. When we finally mount, we will move our right hand to the pommel as our right leg swings over the back of the saddle.

Do not swing your right leg over the horse at this point. Do not get all the way on.

Reach over with your right hand and pet the horse. Reassure him. Rub his neck, and talk to him if you are so inclined. "Good boy." Rub his rear end. This is important, for in the act of mounting, or dismounting, it's possible that your right leg may brush against his rear. If he is unaccustomed to feeling this pressure against him, he could jump out from underneath you.

Don't stay halfway up for too long. We do not want the horse to move off, so it is important that we get down from the horse *before* he moves, not after. If the horse does start to walk off, don't worry about it. At least he isn't bucking.

Most people get into trouble getting up and down. So we want to get above the horse as quickly as we can. The more we hang off one side of him, the more he will want to move underneath us in order to relieve the pressure he is feeling.

A lot of horses blow up when riders dismount, so as you get off, rotate your back and step down toward the front so you don't get nailed. When you are stepping down, turn the horse to you by pulling on the left rein.

Step up. Step down. Repeat. Do this as many times as necessary, making sure that the horse is relaxed.

Repeat the above steps on the horse's right side. Go halfway up, placing your full weight in the right stirrup, pet, and step down.

*Standing in the left stirrup, reach over and pet the horse
to reassure him.*

Repeat until the horse is comfortable with this movement.

Once the horse is pretty relaxed, then we are ready to ride him. The decision to mount the horse should be made on the ground.

The First Ride

It should not be decided when we are halfway up, because, at that point, we have stopped our motion and the act of starting a new movement could startle the horse. Again, the horse tells us what we should do. If we are not comfortable getting on him, then we shouldn't do it.

Once we decide we are going to go all the way up, we will put in our minds that we are getting on the most broke horse in the world. We will not be tentative or wishy-washy in our movements. When we do get on, we need to do it very quickly. We don't want to hesitate halfway up and then get the rest of the way on. We'll mount this horse just as we mount any other horse. If we usually get on rough, we'll get on rough today. If we always kick the horse on the rump when we mount, we'll do so this first time too. Otherwise ten days from now when we are more comfortable with the horse, we'll revert to our routine way of mounting and in so doing we may scare the horse.

Square the horse before mounting. This means that his weight is evenly distributed on all four feet, putting him at his best stance physically to bear your weight.

Now, without hesitation, mount the horse. Place your left foot in the stirrup and swing your right leg up and over his back, but do not put your right foot in the stirrup at this point. Let it hang beside the stirrup.

Pet the horse.

Now get off without hesitation. If you get off slowly, especially if you have been on the horse for a while, there is a good chance you will scare him.

Congratulations! You've just completed your first trail ride, and it was perfect!

So what have we done? We've gotten on this horse that has never before been ridden. While it's been pretty exciting for us, what's been going through the horse's mind? What kind of questions does he have?

"Holy mackerel! What is this thing on my back? Am I gonna have to carry this creature around with me for the rest of my life, to eat with it, and sleep with it?"

And how have we answered?

We've answered the horse's question by getting off of him. A few minutes ago, he didn't know we could get on his back. Then, when we were on, he had no idea that we would get off. So we've done both. By our dismounting before there's a wreck, the horse has learned that we can get off him, as well as on him. Now he's probably saying, "Whew! Is that all he wanted?"

Get on and off many times. Be sure to mount from both sides so it won't be a big deal to the horse if it becomes necessary for you to mount from the right, or off, side.

We'll move on to riding the horse in a minute, but let's talk about that one horse who may buck when you first mount him.

THE BUCKING HORSE

How we address the problem of the bucking horse depends to a large extent on when he bucks.

If, as we put our foot in the stirrup in any position (from having our right foot on the ground to standing up in the stirrup), the horse starts to move off or buck, we'll step down and quickly bring the horse's head back to us.

If as we step up on him, he begins to crow-hop around, then he is telling us that we are moving too fast in our training and that we must go back a step or two in our conditioning.

If the horse starts bucking after we are in the saddle, then we want to pick his head up to the left and pet him. As soon as he quits bucking, we need to let up on the rein, and step down off him.

Now we repeat the lesson of stepping on and off him.

If the horse throws us, we need to pet him, and start the process all over again from the beginning. We need to make sure he is comfortable with each step before we move on to the next.

If the horse throws us, it does not mean that he is going to continue throwing us over and over again. We do not need to chase him, or scold him, or yank him. That won't help anything.

What will help is making sure that the horse understands and is comfortable with each step of the training before we move on to the next.

THE FIRST RIDE

We have been on and off the horse many times now. He knows we can get on. And off. So this time we are going to stay on him for a little ride, and with our right foot in the stirrup.

I am only a guest in my horse's house. I will compare this to my coming to your home for dinner. I knock on your door, and you answer it, inviting me in. We chat for a few minutes before you excuse yourself to check on something in the oven. When you return, I am gone. You find me in your bedroom going through your drawers. You have trusted me in your house, and how have I responded? Am I a gracious guest? Are you a happy host? The answer to both questions is no. So let's remember that at this point, we are guests in our horse's house.

The slower we go here, the faster we will reach our goal.

If the horse starts to walk off once we are in the saddle, we will not pull on the reins, we'll just let him walk. All we need from him right now is for him to relax and to carry us around the pen. We don't have to guide him. It's not important where he goes or if he stands still. Pet the horse whether he walks or just stands.

We don't need to panic if the horse starts walking, trotting, or cantering. We ride a lot of horses that do just that. The hardest thing to control on this first ride is ourselves. If the horse is traveling too fast, pet him to encourage him to slow down. If he bucks we'll want to redirect his movement by picking up the rein and asking the horse to turn.

Let the horse wander around the pen, picking those places he wants to go. This is one big advantage of the round pen. The horse cannot run away with us. He cannot jump any fences or take us under any trees. Since we do not have to worry about where he is going, we do not have to pull on his mouth, and we can concentrate on training him. This first ride is supposed to be boring, we don't want to be in a major wreck. We will give the horse a loose rein, one long enough that he can put his head on the ground if he wants to. If he puts his head down, do not jerk it up. His action does not necessarily mean he is going to buck, he may just be sniffing dirt.

We also don't want to kick the horse with our legs. If we do, six out of ten horses will just trot off, but four out of ten simply won't put up with that nonsense. The horse, at this point, does not understand that our kicking on his sides means for him to move. He just thinks we are beating up on him.

If the horse rolls with you on him, or tries to, pull his head up. If you cannot prevent his going down, step off of him. You do not want to stay on the horse if he rolls. If you do stay on, the odds are eighty percent that when the green horse gets back up, he will begin bucking. Step off. Let him roll, and start again.

If the horse begins to back fast, do not pick up his reins. He is in a prime position to rear, and pressure on the reins will only encourage him to do so. The horse is backing up because he is afraid. We need to let him know that it is all right for us to be on his back. Pet him and reassure him.

As we ride the horse around the pen, we need to pay attention to the humbling feeling flooding our body. We are *so* grateful that this creature is not bucking us off. Remember this moment, for it is a role reversal for all of the times we'll put the bit in the horse's mouth and he will be thinking, "Jiminy Christmas, please don't pull on my mouth, please don't hurt me."

GIVING TO THE BIT

Now we are up on the horse and he has been walking around the round pen at his own pace, choosing his own direction. He has become fairly comfortable with our being up there, and we are also relaxing. We can now begin teaching him that the reins control his front end. If we point his nose to the right, he will go right. If we point it to the left, he will go left.

We will begin by picking up on the left rein and, very gradually, building and holding steady pressure. This giving of the head is very important, for we are not strong enough to pull the horse around if he is excited. The horse has several options at this point. He can move his head to the left, to the right, up, down, forward, or backward. What we want is what the horse does naturally. We want him to be relaxed as he drops his head and tips his nose in to us in the same way he naturally does when he eats dinner or swats

The First Ride

flies. When the horse dips his head in the direction we are asking him for, we will reward him by releasing all of the pressure.

We will be using round reins with a knot in them. Both of our hands will slide on the same side of the knot. Bracing our hands against the saddle will let us feel the horse give to the bit. We will be sliding the reins gradually between our hands and the swell of the saddle.

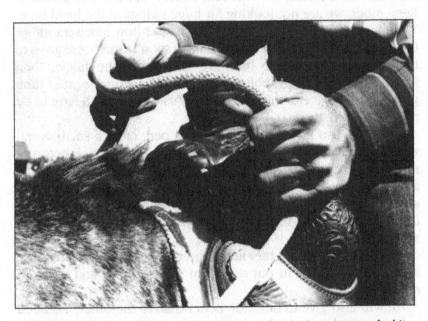

Bracing our hands against the saddle will let us feel the horse give to the bit.

We will not pick up the reins unless we are asking for something, and we will release them immediately once the horse gives us what we want.

We will not jerk or pull the horse's head around. Remember, we are teaching the horse that when we pick up the rein, he must respond by a give of his head. If we get this response, we will then have control.

We will pick the rein up and put light pressure on it. The natural tendency for the horse (and us), is to resist pressure. That is why the horse pulls against us when we pull on the reins. In order to teach our horse the correct response to the pull of the reins, we must first understand why he will want to respond correctly. The reason is that he will want relief. Relief from the bit in his mouth, which is being moved by our pulling on the reins. We can put the horse's head in the correct position by releasing him when he does what we have asked.

We need to keep our hands moving slowly, not fast. When we see slack in the rein, we will immediately release our pressure. Remember, we are not looking for huge swings of the head here. We want the horse to give to us, no matter how small an effort. Once we get that, we will build on it. As soon as the horse gives to the bit, we will release him. We will praise the horse, then mentally count to ten, before repeating the exercise, this time getting him to give to the other side. This exercise will have to be repeated many times.

It should also be done in the round pen, or in a small corral where distractions are limited, as a warm-up exercise before a ride. This is much the same as the stretching exercises that an athlete will do before he participates in his sport. Horses need the same type of warm-up time to get into a learning and attentive frame of mind. Allowing for this time will make things easier on us and the horse.

The horse will get lighter and lighter, on less and less pressure, if we are consistent in our timing of when to pull and when to release.

He will also give to one side better than to the other. We need to know which way the horse gives best, so if we get into trouble and need to pull him around, we can go for that side. We must train him to give equally to the left and to the right before we ask him to run or stop, or we may find ourselves in trouble. The longer we spend teaching this one little lesson, the safer we will be. If we teach it well, tomorrow afternoon we can ride the horse in a parade.

We will give the horse a warning every time we pick up the reins. By picking up the rein along the neck we are cueing him that we are about to make a request.

It is important that we start easy, then gradually increase the pressure until we get the response that we want. We will be using

The First Ride

As the horse gives to the bit, he will drop his nose and soften his neck.

one rein or the other, and we will never pull on both reins at the same time.

As we begin to teach the horse to give to the bit, it is not important to have him move his feet. It is enough that he gives us his head. Once he has learned that, his feet will quickly follow. It is also not important whether the horse's head is up or down, as long as he is giving to the bit.

We will not be using our legs on the green horse. The reins will control the front end of the animal. If we use our legs along with the reins, then we are wasting one of our tools. We can use our legs to mean something else. Later on in our training we will use our legs to tell our horse, "move your feet."

If, when we pick up the reins nice and slowly, the horse fiddles with his head and does not give his head to us quietly and softly, then we are not ready to move on in his training. He must be relaxed.

If we teach the horse correctly, then we will never need to use a bit stronger than a snaffle. This process of learning to give may take twenty to thirty minutes. It is time well spent.

BITTING UP A HORSE

I am frequently asked about bitting up a horse by tying his head around to various parts of the saddle. I don't believe in it. If I tie your arm behind your back, it doesn't teach you to carry your arm around your back, it just makes your arm sore. Bitting up a horse does the same thing. Tying his head to one side doesn't teach him either to give to the bit, or to feel light pressure and to respond to that pressure when you pull on the bit, it just makes his neck sore. It is really a detriment to learning, because as his neck becomes sore, he becomes unwilling to turn to that side. Furthermore, a certain number of horses will fight this procedure and may even rear over backward. Resistance may also cause a horse to hurt his mouth.

If I can teach a horse to give his head just a little, just a fraction of an inch, I'll release him. There is nothing better for communicating with our horse than our hands. And that's what we are after. Communication. Robots are mechanical and don't communicate. If I am in the house watching television while my horse is throwing a fit because his head is tied around to the saddle, then I'm not learning anything about communication. Getting on the horse and asking him to give to the bit with my hands is less dangerous to both horse and trainer, and the end result is that the horse is learning quicker.

UNDERSTANDING THE USE OF THE REINS

The reins will tell the horse which direction to go. For us to understand the use of the reins, or the purpose of the reins, why we're pulling, and why we're releasing, is one of the most important facets of training a horse.

To understand what the horse wants from us will help us in getting the horse to do what we want him to do. The horse wants us to not pull on his mouth with the reins. If we understand this, then it makes it much simpler for us to know why we are pulling and why we are releasing.

Most of us have a tendency to want to hold the horse's head wherever we'd like him to keep it. In other words, if we want to have the horse's head down, we have a tendency, once he gets his head down, to hold it in that position. But, from the horse's point of view, the truth of the matter is that the reason he moves his head down is because we are pulling on his mouth and he's trying to tell us, "Let go."

To help understand this principle, imagine that someone is holding hands too tightly, and your hand begins to hurt. Your first reaction is to open your own hand to let go of theirs. If this doesn't work, and they don't let go of your hand, the next thing you would do would be to pull away. Just as you are trying to communicate to that person to let go by moving your hand, the horse moves his head in order to tell us to let go of his mouth.

So as the horse begins to move his head in the direction we would like him to move it, what we need to do is to release the pressure on his mouth by releasing the pull on the reins.

The next important principle that we need to understand is riding for response. It is important that we do not ride a fixed object, or, in this case, a fixed horse. If we set a horse's head, then basically we are fixing him in one spot. We can have his head in a perfect Western Pleasure position, pick up on the reins, and the horse can still continue moving forward at too fast a lope. The horse's head is in the correct position, but there's no response in this case as we ask him to slow down. Asking the horse to respond, and understanding that we are always looking for that response, enables us to keep our priorities straight while we are riding.

Before we can get the horse's head in the position that we would like, and before we can get the horse's feet to move in the position that we would like, and at the speed we would like, the horse has to respond. It is mandatory that the horse begins, and ends, each maneuver with this softness.

If we pick up the reins and ask the horse to move his feet, say to the right, and the horse does so, but never softens and relaxes his neck into our hands with the reins, eventually we won't be able to get him to move his feet to the right. So during our training, it will be important that the horse always relaxes into our hands with his mouth, his head, and his neck prior to moving his feet in the direction that we ask him.

HORSE THAT WON'T MOVE AND HORSE THAT WON'T STOP

When I was doing clinics, I found that there were people with one of two problems with their green horses when they were first starting to ride them. The first person said, "Help! I can't get my horse to move." The second one said, "Help! I can't get my horse to stop." We will approach both of these problems in the same way.

On either horse, we'll keep working on him to make sure he is giving to the bit better. Once we are positive that the horse is giving to the bit well, then we'll work on the problem.

We can have the horse look to one side or the other, as we take almost all of the slack out of the rein so the horse has his head, say to the right, but we're holding his head to the right on a loose rein. The horse is going to stand that way for a little while but then he'll try to straighten his neck. When he does so, he'll take the remaining slack out of the right rein and bump the end of it. He will again bend his head to the right. Now he's standing with a loose rein to the right, and he can't get his head completely forward again. As we keep the pressure on his neck, he will eventually get sore and will move his feet to give himself relief. Almost always, if he's looking right, he'll move his left front foot first. Then the right. When the right foot moves, we will release the rein and pet him. This usually solves the problem of the horse that won't move.

If the horse is constantly moving, we'll use the same procedure. We must remember that any time we pick up the rein, we are discouraging movement. We will repeat this process of getting the horse to give, and move, to the left and right, alternating direction of the horse's movement each time. As he turns, he will stop, however briefly. As he stops, ask for the opposite rein. Build on longer and longer stops, praising the horse each time.

HEAD SETS AND SOFT HANDS

I never ride for head set or breaking at the poll. I ride for response. If the horse feels heavy and is laying on the bit, then no matter how well he did the maneuver, I will go back in my training until I'm getting the response I want.

(There are times, in certain classes, when we will want our horse's poll to be at a certain angle. This will be addressed in a later chapter.)

The horse will put his head where we release it. The release is his reason, his reward, for putting it where we ask. No tie-downs or running martingales will work as well as trained hands.

We want to keep our hands on the reins inside the horse's shoulders, so we aren't flapping and waving them about. At no time should they be out farther from our body than our hips. If we don't have any slack in the reins, or if we move our hands too quickly, then we are in danger of becoming heavy handed. When this happens, frequently we would rather blame the horse for his behavior than learn what we are doing to cause his reaction.

Riding light handed means giving the horse the opportunity to work on less. It means having enough slack in the reins and moving our hands slowly enough to give our horse time to respond. We must concentrate on becoming light-handed so that we never inadvertently pull back when the horse gives to us. As we practice letting the horse work on less, soon we won't have to be pulling on his mouth with our hands at all.

THE WORLD OUTSIDE

When the horse is comfortable and soft in his responses, and is giving quietly to the bit, we are ready to take him out into the pasture. We will only move him out of the round pen when we are comfortable with doing so. As we ride him outside, we are teaching him that it's OK to walk around, anywhere, with us on his back. Remember, we are still guests in his house.

Just as the horse found it easier to move in the round pen than in the stall, he will find it easier to move and walk around in the pasture. Once we get him into the National Forest, he'll really have a good time!

Chapter Eight ————

The First Few Rides

B efore we get on the horse for our second ride, we'll put
him through the same steps as we did the first day we got
on him. This review will help us measure how good a job
we've done to this point.

The horse will tell us where we should start today. We'll put
him in the round pen and watch how he runs. Is he as tired as he
was after the first ride? No. He's fresh. We need that energy. We
spend money to put feed for energy in this horse, and if we run
him around it's like pouring gasoline on the ground. We may need
that energy four or five hours later today, and we sure need it in
order to train him. Ideally he should run around the pen for only

one-half or one full turn before he begins to pay attention to us. If he continues to run around the pen ignoring us, then we know we haven't done as good a job in training as we should have for that first ride. If, on the other hand, we see something we like, then that tells us the training method we used worked.

Basically we're just going to check out the horse on each of the steps. We'll start by rubbing him with our hands, then the rope, then the saddle pad, and finally we'll saddle him.

Once we have the saddle on, we'll turn the horse loose in the round pen. Again, all of the work to this point is done without the halter.

If the horse bucks, we'll move him around the pen until he is completely relaxed before we begin to climb on his back. When the horse bucks the first day, it's not important. If, on the second day, he bucks, I'll make a note of it. On the third day, I'll put a halter on him, and if he starts bucking I'll try to discourage him by pulling his head toward me. I don't want the horse to get into thinking he can buck for the first five minutes every time he is saddled. It's important to establish these patterns right away.

We can help the horse relax by having him follow us around the round pen. When we're comfortable that he is relaxed, we'll follow the same sequence we did the first day as far as getting on. After bridling the horse, we'll begin by putting our foot in the left stirrup and then removing it. We'll progress to the point where we're getting halfway up and down on both sides of the horse.

When we feel he is relaxed with what we are doing, we'll go ahead and climb all the way on. We'll get on and off several times. It's important that we not stay up long on our first mounting, thinking, "Gee, I stayed on his back for two hours yesterday, I'm sure it's all right."

Remember, we always want the horse to be relaxed with each step before we move on to the next. When he is relaxed with our getting on and off him, then we'll go through the exercise of having him give to the bit.

When the horse is giving to the bit well and dropping his head well, and you feel relaxed on him, then get off. Walk him out of the round pen to wherever you are going to ride him that day, to the pasture, or to the trail-ride area. Even if the horse has been led with a halter, don't just assume that he'll lead with a bit in his mouth. When you start to walk off leading him, do it gently so you don't jar his mouth.

The longer we ride the horse in the pen, the more bored and less responsive he will become. By taking him to an open area and giving him a job with a purpose, working cattle for example, or weaving through brush, we are giving him a reason to turn left and right. Now he understands why we are asking him for these turns.

Once the horse is relaxed, with the rider in the saddle, and is giving to the bit well, we are ready to take him on a trail ride.

OUTSIDE ON THE TRAIL

Trail riding is a critical component of horse training. You can ride a horse until he is fifteen years old in the ring, and he still may not be safe on the trail. And if he isn't safe on the trail, then he really isn't safe in the ring, or around other horses. For the next few hours, we're going to take the horse on a trail ride. It will be fun for both of us, and we won't ask much of the horse.

We do not want to ride the horse, at this point, in a pasture full of loose horses. He can be taken out with other horses as long as they also are being ridden. If he is in the company of other saddle horses, this makes it easy for the just-broken horse to follow along.

We'll now climb on the horse, and ideally he will walk down the trail or around in the pasture.

As soon as the horse is relaxed with us on the trail, we'll then begin our exercise of having him give to the bit while he is moving forward. Remember, at this point in our training, we have not used our legs on the horse at any time. We do not want to make the mistake of thinking we can get up on this just-broken horse and kick him. Maybe we can, maybe not. Use of our legs will come later.

While the horse may have been giving to the bit and turning his head to the left or to the right on command, he may not have been moving his feet. Now he is responding with his front feet stepping off to the right and to the left. As we keep the horse's mind occupied, we'll keep him out of trouble.

If we'll spend the time to make sure he gives us his head, then we will be in control and we'll be able to take him anywhere on the trail. If the horse decides he wants to act up, and we've taught him to give to the bit, then at least we can decide where to have our rodeo. If we move the horse back and forth, changing directions, then eventually he will get tired of looking for a rodeo site.

Once the horse is giving to the bit well, we'll move him off the trail, and we'll begin to guide him around obstacles. We don't want to be riding a horse for twenty years down the trail and still be riding a green horse. If we keep riding him down a six-inch path, he won't know much more than when we started. So it is better to get off the trail and bend the horse around bushes and trees, such as creosote or mesquite in the desert, aspen if you're in my country. This will also teach us about our timing. If we are turning our horse at an aspen, and he turns two feet past the tree, then we've asked for that turn too late.

These exercises will get us out to the trail and back safely. As you feel you are gaining more control on the horse, your exercise should progress to where you are walking him between objects that are closer together. Next you'll be riding the horse up and down basic natural trail obstacles, as you practice ascents and descents.

As the horse progresses through the various steps of going around obstacles, and up and down different terrain, you can advance him into crossing more difficult trail areas. The quicker you expose the horse to, for example, water or a creek bed, the easier it is for the horse to handle. But, again, do not rush the horse.

Our goals for these first few days on the trail are:

1. The horse accepts his surroundings.
2. The horse learns he can walk and carry us around in a relaxed manner.
3. The horse gives to the bit.
4. The horse goes up and down, and around, different trail obstacles.
5. The horse walks by fearful objects.

6. We begin to gain control over the horse as we get him to go where we want him to go.

FEARFUL OBJECTS

At some point on the trail, we will encounter something that will concern, or even frighten, the horse. Most people teach their horses to overcome their fear of frightening things by having the horse go up to the dreaded object. The horse is then supposed to put his nose on the thing, sniff it, and see that it won't hurt him.

That's pretty ridiculous when you think about it. It takes time, and if I'm in a show, I'll lose the class while my horse is spending his time sniffing frightening objects.

When my horse is afraid of something, I want him to act as though the object isn't there. This means walking by it as though it were invisible.

When he first sees the object, his flight instinct is probably going to take over. He'll want to run away from whatever is scaring him, to turn and escape. I don't want him to do this. Since we've done the "facing fear" lesson (Chapter Four), the horse should face whatever is frightening him.

The first thing we want to do is to forget that the horse spooked at the object, so that we are not concentrating on it.

In dealing with the frightening object, we must consider where we are in the horse's training. If this is our first trail ride, then we are going to have to approach the problem in a different manner than we would if we were on a horse who has been ridden more.

If you are on a very green horse, or are in a situation where you don't have room to circle the horse or to move around, then relax and let the horse stop. When the horse is completely relaxed and you feel that you can ask him to move forward and he will, then ask him to do so. Do not have him put his nose on the object. Your goal is to ride a relaxed horse by the object that has him concerned.

If the horse begins backing, don't try to stop him. Relax and sit there. He will eventually stop. When he does, sit and relax on him for a few minutes and then ask him to move forward. Progress in this manner until you are by the object.

FEARFUL MOVING OBJECTS

Handling frightening objects that move, such as dogs, trucks, cars, cattle, bicycles, four-wheelers and so on, should be handled in a different manner from objects that are stationary.

Obviously if a semi-truck and trailer is coming toward our horse and could possibly scare him to the point where he jumps in front of it, we would be in a great deal more danger than if a bicycle came at the horse. Therefore, our judgement as to whether we are in danger on the horse's back is important. If a car or truck is approaching, and we have doubts as to whether or not the horse may move into its path, then the best solution for us is to get down off the horse and hold him. If at any time we are uncomfortable, we need to dismount. It really doesn't take any brains to get hurt on a horse. It's better to be a live wimp than to stick it out, stay on the horse's back, and end up in the hospital or dead.

In the case where we feel we can maintain our safety and control of the horse, we can stay on him and have him turn and face the moving object. As the object goes by, we'll continue having the horse watch it until it is out of sight. If we are dealing with dogs, it is best to have the horse turn and face the dogs until he relaxes or the dogs leave.

THE HORSE TROTS

There will be times when the horse wants to trot spontaneously. For the first trot, we're not going to kick him into it, we're just going to let him do it. It's his decision. This is important, for it teaches the horse that it's all right for him to trot with us on his back.

When the horse trots spontaneously, let him go for fifteen or twenty steps and then pick up on the rein that he gives to the easiest. Turn him 180 degrees and have him slow to a walk. If he relaxes and slows to the walk, then the next time he picks up the trot, have him trot a little farther, as long as he feels relaxed and you are comfortable.

All of the gaits are all right on these first few rides, as long as the horse feels relaxed underneath you as you ride him, and as long as you are not kicking him into any of them. They should be the horse's idea. If the horse is comfortable and wants to canter, I'll let him go into it for four or five strides, and then turn him and walk. It is important at the canter that we not let the horse accelerate his speed or we may get into trouble.

TEACHING THE HORSE TO SLOW DOWN AND STOP

We have to teach the horse to slow down before we can teach him to stop.

If we are riding a horse that's giving us lots of energy and lots of movement, we need to first recognize that this is exactly what we need in order to teach him both to stop and to give to the bit. As long as the horse isn't bucking, then we're all right.

If we're riding a hot-blooded horse that wants to move, it's much easier to progress faster in our training in particular exercises than it is if we are on a horse that just slowly and calmly walks down the trail.

So our horse for this example is trotting, and we're not sure if we have control. We do not want the horse to build into the canter and then into the run and get him, or us, scared.

The horse is trotting with us, and we would feel more comfortable with him walking. What do we do?

We'll let him trot in a straight line for twenty to thirty yards. Now we'll turn him a sharp 180-degree turn to the right. It's important that the horse does make a 180-degree turn, and that it is an abrupt turn, not a circle. Right after the turn, the horse will take at least one step at a walk before he breaks back into his trot. When you get that one step at the walk, release the reins.

If the horse begins to trot off again, let him go fifteen or twenty yards before asking him to make a 180-degree turn in the opposite direction. If you turned him to the right the first time, turn him to the left the second time. This means that the horse is going up and down in a straight line, instead of making a circle. It also insures that the horse actually has a stop, however brief.

Do this as many times as it takes, until, when the horse makes a turn, he breaks down into a walk and continues walking. Don't become impatient with the horse if he continues to trot, even if he doesn't walk at all the first couple of hours, just continue the exercise.

If the horse has been moving for three hours, and you give him the opportunity to stop, he probably will. Eventually he will learn that when you pick up the reins, he's to stop going in one direction. He'll anticipate stopping, and will stand still for longer periods of time.

When you feel the horse begin to stop, you need to relax your body completely to make sure that you are not subconsciously asking him to move again.

HORSE REFUSING TO GO IN DIRECTION YOU HAVE CHOSEN

In this example, we'll deal with the horse who does not want to go in the direction you have chosen.

Move the horse fifteen steps in another direction. Turn him 180 degrees. Move him another fifteen steps. Turn him 90 degrees in another direction. Move fifteen steps. Turn 90 degrees. Fifteen steps. Turn. You get the idea. If he wants to trot during this exercise, that's all right. The principle here is to keep him moving. It is important that the horse cannot escape going in the direction you have chosen, by resting. Pretty soon he'll be saying, "Jiminy Christmas, why can't I just walk down the trail in *that* direction?"

The first few rides are spent practicing these exercises. As with everything else in our training program, the horse tells us how fast we can progress to the next steps.

Chapter Nine

Ground Training

|T| o teach the horse basic ground manners, whether we are picking up his feet, clipping his ears, giving him a bath, or doing any other work we do on him from the ground, we will use the same principles that we employed when we taught him the round-pen and the facing-fear lessons (Chapter Two, Chapter Four).

PICKING UP THE HORSE'S FEET

At this point, we can have the horse turn and face us when we walk into the round pen.

Begin by standing to the side of the horse and toward the front of him. We will not try to pick up his foot as long as he is resisting us.

Again, the principle of starting with small steps and gradually working up to the achievement of our goal is important. In terms of picking up a horse's feet, this means that we might start by rubbing his shoulder, and then petting his head to let him know that all we wanted to do was to just rub him. Then we will rub our hands down his front leg in stages, each time returning to his head and petting him.

If at any point, he reacts violently by striking or rearing, return to working him on the fence and doing our round-pen work. The only time during this lesson that we should go back to working the horse on the fence is when we feel we are in danger. Cultivate patience, and always remember to give the horse the benefit of the doubt. It is also important that we give him as many opportunities as possible to stand still.

If you send the horse back to the round-pen lesson you may find that it will not take too much work to get him to cooperate. It may require only a turn or two around the pen to develop his "want to" attitude.

If the horse has not offered any violent behavior, but you are not comfortable in rubbing your hand over his leg, you can rub his leg lightly with a coiled rope, in the manner outlined in Chapter Five.

After he becomes used to our rubbing his shoulder, we will rub farther and farther down the horse's leg, to the knee, then return and pet his head, to the cannon-bone area, return and pet the head, and so on, until we can touch around the hoof area.

The next step will be to get the horse to shift his weight to the opposite front leg. We can get this weight shift just by pushing on him gently with our shoulder, then releasing the pressure of our shoulder as soon as he leans. If we keep leaning on him, he'll begin to lean back.

When we can consistently get him to rock his weight back and forth, and we think that we can get him to actually lift the leg that we want to pick up, then we will pick it up for a split second. Once we can get the horse to let us hold his leg up for a second, we will put it back down. We will then lift it and hold it for a second or two longer before putting it back down, and so on. It is important that we always return the leg to the ground *before* the horse asks us to do so. Eventually we will be able to lift each of his front legs and hold them up. When we are at this point, we can use a hoof pick to clean the hoof and to tap lightly on the foot and sole to accustom the horse to a shoer tapping in the nails.

After this sequence is complete with both front feet, we're ready to go to the rear legs. For this example, we will use the horse's left rear leg. When working with the hind feet, I put a halter on the horse, with the halter rope over the horse's back so the end of the lead rope is on the opposite side of the horse to the one I am working on.

We'll again begin by rubbing the horse with the coiled lariat. We may have to start at his hip and rub him, then pet his head, and progress in stages all the way down to the hoof. If the horse starts to kick at us, or at the coiled lariat, we can use a buggy whip to rub down his back leg. The purpose of the whip is to put distance between us and the horse. There is no need to hit the horse with the buggy whip, for he will eventually get tired of kicking, especially when he finds out that we are not grabbing him, and that there is nothing to fear. When he quits kicking at the buggy whip, rub him down with the lariat, then with your hands.

Once the horse has accepted the rubbing of his rear legs, we are ready to go on to the next step.

Have the horse step back until the hind leg that is closest to you, is stepping up toward his front leg. Once the horse is in that position, place yourself so your left leg is between his front legs. This way, if the horse moves forward, he will push you out of his way. Your left hand should hold the lead rope. The rope should be loose enough so that the horse is not bent toward the side you are on, yet without any slack. Your left hand should also grasp his mane. This helps you maintain your body position close to the horse and keeps your face close to his side, hopefully out of danger from his back feet. I know this position sounds awkward, and it is the first few times you try it, but it is also the safest way to pick up a horse's back feet.

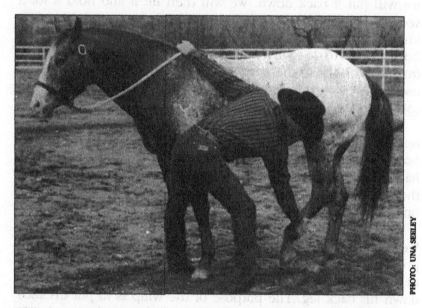

While this may look awkward, it is the safest way to pick up a horse's back foot.

We'll begin building toward picking up the back leg by just touching the hip and returning and petting the horse's head. Continue in this manner until your hand is at the back of the gaskin muscle. At this point, begin applying pressure with your right hand, bringing the horse's leg forward. If he begins to kick, do not reprimand him. Stand up and pet him, and then reposition the horse and yourself and begin again.

Continue in this manner until you can lift the hoof off the ground with your hand on the horse's gaskin muscle without the horse getting upset or kicking. You will have the foot up off the ground only for a split second. Then pet the horse. Repeat, each time increasing the length of time the horse's hoof is off the ground. When you can keep the hoof off the ground for ten seconds, you are ready to move on, or, in this case, down.

Next we will go down the leg past the hock. Slide your hand just past the hock, and begin the same procedure by picking up the leg and putting it back down.

Keep advancing in this manner until you can pick up the leg at the pastern. Once this can be accomplished, hold the bottom of the hoof in your right hand and move it a few inches to the outside, or away from the horse, to see if the horse is relaxed.

It is important throughout this entire procedure to return often to the horse's head and pet him. Do not hold the leg up too long at any one time. We always want to put the leg down *prior* to the horse's pulling it away.

Once you feel that the horse is comfortable with your handling his feet when you are standing with your left leg between his front legs, you can begin moving out to his side and progress to moving the leg backward toward the rear of the horse. In order to accomplish this, you will have to move your left leg from between the horse's front legs. As you do so, remember to stay close to the side of the horse.

After we can take the leg straight back and the horse is completely relaxed with it, then we'll move toward the front of him and again place our left leg in between his two front legs. We will pick up the horse's hind leg a few inches off the ground, holding it with our left hand, as we begin tapping on the side of the hoof with our hoof pick.

Once the horse is relaxed with this handling of his left rear leg, we are ready to repeat the lesson on his right side.

CLIPPING

Rather than having the horse jump, and having us drop a hundred-dollar pair of electric clippers in the dirt and becoming upset, it's easier to start with a cheaper cordless vibrator and throw it, when it is not running, in the horse's trough while he is eating. This is starting with a small step. We can then advance to having the vibrator on while he is eating. The next step would be to take him to the round pen. Start rubbing him with the vibrator beginning with his nose and advancing from there to the side of his face, to his neck and on up to his ears.

In handling a horse's ears, if he is either shy of our hand or the vibrator, it is best to remember that our goal is to be able to touch the ears without the horse moving his head. Therefore if the horse is ducking his head in three seconds, we will only want to leave our hand on his ears for less than two seconds, or in this case, the vibrator. Dealing with the head-shy, or ear-shy, horse is covered in Chapter Five.

Always stop and pet the horse whenever he makes any type of improvement during any part of the training program. If at any one stage the horse is rebelling too much, return to the stage where he was comfortable with the vibrator, and begin again from there.

Once the horse will accept the vibrator on and around his nose and around his ears, progress to the clippers. You can start accustoming the horse to ear clippers before you move on to the larger models. Turn them on and do the back of the ears, at first, just holding the clippers against the ear without actually cutting the hair. Continue in this manner until you can clip the inside of the horse's ears.

As you work with the clippers, make sure they do not overheat and burn the horse's muzzle or ears.

Getting the horse used to having his ears clipped may take several hours, so set aside a day in your training program to teach the horse to accept this procedure. It is best not to resort to tying the horse up, or twitching him, or using any type of restraint. Remember as you are working through this problem, you are not solving it for a day, but for a lifetime.

BATHING

The simplest way to get the horse used to having a bath is to turn him loose in a good strong corral or round pen and turn the hose on. The water pressure shouldn't be so powerful that it will hurt the horse, yet it should be enough so that you can get ten to fifteen feet away and still be able to squirt him.

Do not squirt the horse in the face. Any horse will accept water running over his face as long as he is not irritated by water being squirted directly into his ears, eyes, or nose. There should be no force behind the water when you are doing the horse's face.

Gradually work the hose closer and closer to the horse until you can finally hose him off all over. Start at the legs and work up.

Another simple solution that is safe for both the horse and the trainer, is to put a halter with a cotton lead rope on the horse and stand in the middle of the corral holding the rope. Let the horse move around you as you squirt his legs and then gradually move up to the rest of his body.

Both of these methods are much safer than tying a horse in the wash rack or tying him to a post for his first bath. If we've done our job correctly, getting him used to the stream of water, we should have no trouble giving him subsequent baths.

LONGEING

We can teach any halter-broken horse to longe in a short period of time. A gaited horse is the hardest to teach to longe, because his feet move differently. Too much longeing of a gaited horse isn't good, as it changes the natural way he places his feet, and he may get into bad habits.

When longeing a horse, we always want to be careful not to work a young horse too long, or any horse too hard or in deep, sandy soil. Whenever you feel as though your horse is getting tired, or if you are in doubt, let him stop and rest. You can use these resting moments by working on verbal cues such as "Back" and "Come." Also, when longeing, be sure to work the horse equally in both directions.

To teach a horse to longe, we will begin by using a six-foot rope attached to the horse's halter. We will hold the lead a foot or two from the bullsnap, and in the other hand, we'll hold a four-foot buggy whip. The horse will be positioned between the lead, at his front, and the whip, at his rear, making a triangle with us at the top of it.

We will stand to the side of the horse and ask him to walk around us, by tapping high on his hip, not on his back or his rump. We will keep slack in the lead. It is important that we watch the inside hind leg, or the leg closest to us, as well as the horse's flank, for this will give us an indication of whether or not the horse is thinking about kicking us. We will be turning as the horse turns.

If we think the horse is going to try to kick with his hind leg, we will pull firmly on the halter rope, pulling his nose in to us and forcing his rear end away, hopefully taking us out of kicking range.

By teaching a horse to longe in this fashion, we are also teaching him control. Having the horse flying around us, going ninety miles per hour at the end of a thirty-foot rope is not a controlled exercise.

We'll begin teaching this control by asking the horse to walk around us at a distance of two or three feet. As the horse becomes consistent at this distance, we will let the rope slip through our hands, giving him more rope to get farther away from us. The horse is like a dance partner. If he's not relaxed or not paying attention, then we need to practice until he is.

We will send him out to four or five feet. When he's consistent here, we will ask him to trot. We will "kiss" to the horse to get him to increase his speed. If he does not quicken his pace, we may have to tap him lightly on the hip with the whip while making the kissing sound. If the horse turns and faces us, wanting to stop, we will shorten up on the lead rope and again go to the closer-in exercises.

While longeing a horse, there are several reasons we should never let him pull on the rope, or take the slack completely out of it. First, it teaches the horse to pull against us. Second, it pulls the horse off balance, putting more weight on his inside front leg, which creates a tendency to cause damage to both the hoof and the tendon.

When I feel a horse pull on me, I'm going to pull on him. Hard. If the horse is going around us, and we feel him pull, then we are teaching him to do exactly that if we do nothing about it. If he's pulling, increase the pressure on the rope until the horse either gives to the pressure, or comes to a stop. If he stops, shorten the lead rope and begin longeing him again. Remember, the horse should never be out of control and moving as fast, or as slow, as he wants to move. We control his speed, and as he is moving around, he should be listening to us.

For the horse to longe correctly at twenty feet, he must first longe correctly at three feet. If he pulls on the rope at three feet, he is going to pull on it more at twenty feet, so we should solve any longeing problems while the horse is still close to us.

The only exception to this rule will be at the canter. The horse should be no closer than fifteen feet from us at the canter. Cantering is a more advanced manuever in longeing, so it's important to get the walk and the trot down first.

If we want to teach our horse verbal commands, longeing is a good place to begin. We can start by repeating a verbal cue over and over while the horse is in a particular gait. It is important that we inforce each verbal cue given. For example, if the horse is at the trot and we give the verbal cue to walk, we will count two seconds before tugging on the lead rope and getting the horse back to the walk. In training the horse, we should always wait two seconds after a verbal cue is given before we do anything physical. If we don't, the horse will work off of the physical cue, rather than the verbal one.

To teach the horse to back up on a verbal cue, we stand at his side, facing him and holding the lead six inches below the bullsnap. We hold a stiff dressage whip in the other hand and say the word "back," then wait two seconds before tapping him below the knees on the front legs with the whip. Once he takes a step back, stop and pet him. Repeat this process until the horse begins backing when you give the verbal cue.

To teach the horse to come to us on command, we use about a ten-foot rope. We give the verbal cue "Come," count off two seconds, and then pull on the rope, repeating the process until the horse comes to us when asked.

Once the horse understands the verbal command to come, we can increase the speed at which he comes to us by using the techniques outlined in Chapter Two. We will call him and then step to the side. We will ask him to hurry by throwing the rope at his rear end as we continue stepping aside. This will improve both his performance and his speed.

GROUND-TYING

When training our horse to ground-tie, we will use a halter and a ten- to fifteen-foot rope. We will begin by teaching the horse the verbal command "Whoa" by walking alongside him saying "Whoa," and then pulling down on the lead rope.

Once the horse begins stopping well and understands our verbal command, then we will back away from him a few steps. If he starts to come toward us, we will say "Whoa" and flick the rope, bumping his chin with the bullsnap of the lead. The horse should stop and stand still.

We will progress in this manner, getting farther and farther away from the horse and having him stand longer and longer before we return to him and pet him.

Each time the horse starts to move off before we return to him, we will pick up the rope, pull on it hard, and bump him on the chin with the bullsnap.

Once the horse understands the verbal commands of "Come" and "Back" he will have the foundation he needs to learn to ground-tie. When we ground-tie him, he should wait for us in the spot where we left him.

To further the training of the horse, and his understanding of ground-tying, we'll put some feed in front of him. We will walk away from him, and if he moves for the feed, we will say "Whoa" and pull on the rope. To advance the horse even further, we'll move him out of the arena and put him in a grassy area. Again, if the horse begins to eat, we'll regain his attention by pulling on the rope.

ACCEPTING ROPES AND WIRE AROUND HIS LEGS

To teach the horse to accept either hobbles or ropes around his legs, or to stand still if he gets caught up in wire, it is easiest to start in the round pen.

We will begin with both the saddle and a halter with a long rope attached to it on the horse. We will attach a second rope with a soft lay to the saddle horn and flip it around and over the horse's rump and down by his hind legs so the horse gets used to that feeling. In this manner, we are beginning to teach the horse to put up with the rope.

If he gets scared and begins to run, we'll pull on the halter rope and have the horse turn and face us. Only after the horse is calm will we begin again.

We'll proceed in this manner until the rope that is attached to the saddle horn can be draped all around the horse and wrapped around his legs without his objecting. If at any time the horse gets tangled up in the rope, we'll let go of it so he won't get hurt. If he's been taught the lesson correctly, the chances are that if he ever gets caught in wire, he will stand calmly until freed.

HOBBLES

Never put a rope on the horse's hind legs to hobble him.

I don't use hobbles on both front legs, because I've had a few horses outrun me wearing them. I use a one front leg hobble, which is very effective. I've never had a horse get a rope burn with this system. The horse is even able to lie down and roll without getting into trouble.

To teach a horse to accept this restraint, put him in the round pen with a rope tied around the pastern of one front leg. You will hold the other end of the rope as you step away from him.

At first he will strike and pull at the rope, and at this point you will put only mild pressure on it. As soon as the horse quits striking at the rope, release all pressure. As he accepts the rope and stands quiet with all his feet on the ground, begin adding just a little bit of pressure and then releasing it before he reacts.

As the horse leaves his hobbled foot on the ground for longer and longer periods of time, and accepts more pressure on the rope, you then begin pulling on the rope enough so that you can lift the horse's front leg off to the side. When he will let you move his front leg, put still more pressure on the rope so that he takes a step toward you.

Once you can lead him around with the rope attached to his

leg, send him off at a trot around the round pen without putting pressure on the rope. As he's trotting around the pen, begin slowly adding pressure until he stops and faces you.

When you can move the horse's leg around without his fighting you, you are ready to stake him out. You will use a one-leg front hobble, or take a two-leg hobble and cut it in half. Be sure to have at least four swivel points between the horse's foot and the stake. If you don't, as the horse walks around, he will twist the rope into such a cat's cradle that you will have to cut the whole mess. So put a double swivel on the hobble, put another swivel on the end of the rope that will be attached to the hobble, put a swivel on the opposite end of the rope, and finally, a swivel on the stake in the ground. The swivels will insure that the rope does not get tangled up. Also make sure there aren't any stakes, trees, or stumps in the area accessible to the horse that he could get tangled up in.

When first staking out a horse, use no more than ten to fifteen feet of rope. In this way, if the horse does get excited and starts to run, he can't get up a full head of steam before pressure is put on his front leg.

A tether, or picket, line is also a good method for tying a horse up for long periods of time. The line should be at least nine to ten feet in the air, well over the horse's head. The lead line should be long enough so that the horse's head can reach the ground.

POLE EXERCISE

This exercise can be done in the first three or four days of training a horse. It can also be done with yearlings.

The pole exercise helps develop the horse's eye/foot coordination. It is a good exercise for a young horse, for it not only teaches him where his feet are, but it helps him carry his weight in a more balanced manner. It will also, as we progress up to the canter, increase the horse's ability to work off his hindquarters.

We'll need five to seven poles about twelve to fifteen feet long. One end of the pole will be rested on the bottom rail of the round pen. Since pens vary, that bottom rail may be one to two feet above the ground, which will elevate one end of the pole to that height. The other end of the pole will lie on the ground inside. The poles should run all the way around the pen like spokes of a wheel, but with different distances between them. The distance between the first and second pole might be seven feet, with ten feet between the second and third pole, and so on.

I use lightweight poles. They are cylinders that carpet has been rolled up on, and I wrap them in duct tape. They're inexpensive, and they won't hurt the horse if he hits them. This is especially good for a young horse jumping the poles, because when he hits one it won't hurt nearly as badly as a heavy, wooden pole.

Our goal is to get the horse to trot over the poles without touching them with his feet while keeping up a constant speed.

We will start by moving the horse around the round pen. He will have a tendency to cut to the inside, toward the lower end of the poles. We'll let him move over the poles at that place until he is comfortable. Then we will ask him to move out farther away from the center of the round pen and closer to the higher end of the poles until he is consistent at both going over the poles and maintaining an even trot.

It will take several days with this exercise to get the horse to where he is not bumping his legs or his feet into the poles. With practice, there will be a tremendous difference in the way the horse moves, in the way he turns, and in his overall performance.

As the horse progresses, we can ask him to do the same exercise at the slow lope until he is comfortable at that speed.

We will then introduce turns. We will ask the horse to turn between poles, continuing his lope as he does so. When he is comfortable with this, we will lift the poles to where both ends are even, that is, we will lift the end of the pole that has been on the ground up to a height that matches the end resting on the bottom rail of the round pen.

We will ask the horse to trot over the jumps, and then we'll progress to the canter. One of the things we are trying to accomplish with this exercise is to get the horse to work off his hindquarters. After he makes his jump at the canter, and his back feet have landed on the other side of the pole, we'll have him change directions as quickly as possible. As he changes directions, he will pivot on his hindquarters and elevate his front end as he goes back over the pole.

This can be practiced throughout the horse's lifetime. If you don't have time to ride, or can't ride, it's a fun exercise to do with your horse.

CROSSING A TARP OR PLASTIC

To get the horse used to plastic, or to get him over a scary object, such as a trail bridge, we need to begin in the round pen. We can bring in a tarp or a trail bridge and place it right by the fence of the pen. We can also apply the principles outlined here to loading a horse that is not halter broken into a trailer.

Lay the opened-out tarp along the edge of the fence. Begin by moving the horse around the round pen. Our goal is to convince him that the best possible place for him to be in the pen is on the tarp. As the horse goes by the tarp several times, he will more than likely cut to the inside so he does not have to step on the awful thing.

For the first several trips around the pen, let the horse cut to the inside and go by the tarp. Don't try to make him step on it or go over it.

Once the horse is going by the tarp comfortably, we will progress in our training. While we can't stop the horse from running, we can decide from which direction he'll cross the tarp. As an example, in this case he will cross it from the left.

Let's say the tarp is at twelve o'clock. As the horse comes toward it and begins to cut to the inside, we will turn him back to the right as quickly as possible. As the horse turns back to the right and keeps moving, we will turn him back to the left again as he reaches five o'clock. Essentially what we are doing is confining him to a little less than half of the round pen. We are asking him to stay on one side of it. We will continue in this manner, turning the horse back and forth between twelve and five o'clock, only allowing him to stand still when he is facing the tarp.

The horse might stand still but he might be facing either us or away from the tarp. Since we would not want him to stand very long in this position, we would move him as quickly as possible, or annoy him to get him to turn and face in the direction of the tarp. The distance that he is from the tarp is not important, only that he stands and faces in its direction.

Once we have accomplished this—say he is at five o'clock, thirty feet from the tarp and facing it—the longer we let him stand there, the easier it is going to be for us to get him to move in the direction of the tarp when we do ask him to move.

As he relaxes and calms down at this distance, then we will begin to ask him to move again, toward the tarp. It's important that we have him calm at each level before moving him on to the next.

When we ask him to move toward the tarp, ideally he will take a half step, or a full one. If he does this, we will stop asking him to move forward and let him rest for just a minute or two. We can proceed with this, asking him to move a step or two toward the tarp and then backing off, until he moves closer and is within a few feet of it.

Eventually the horse is going to be next to the tarp, standing still. We'll let him rest here for a minute before we ask him to move. When we make our request, he will either cut to the inside to miss the tarp, or he will jump over the corner of it, again, cutting to the inside. In either case, as he cuts to the inside, we'll turn him as quickly as we can to get him back on the right side of the clock, facing the tarp again. We'll then repeat the process.

If at any point in the training the horse begins to put a foot on the tarp, or in the direction of the tarp, we will immediately back off and let him rest. Our goal is not just to get the horse over the tarp, or into the trailer, but to have him stand on the tarp, or in the trailer, *calmly*. Therefore, he must be calm throughout the training process. If we are working on getting a horse in the back of a trailer, it is even more important to give the horse more time to relax in between our requests for him to move.

Eventually the horse will be standing calmly with one front foot, then two, on the tarp. The longer we wait at these intervals, the easier it is going to be to get the horse back to this position if he becomes scared and begins to run again. Now the horse is beginning to associate the tarp with a place to rest.

This exercise also gets the horse used to walking over things.

How did we do? Did we pull on our horse? Kick him? Spur him? Were we safe? Was he? Was he calmer after the lesson?

OVERCOMING FEAR OF THE WORMING SYRINGE

Getting a horse to overcome his fear of any particular object on the ground, such as the worming syringe, requires us to go through a thinking process in order to break down a teaching process that will explain to him that he does not have to be afraid.

It's not really the taste of the wormer that the horse objects to. Generally, he objects to an unusual object being forced into his mouth and to having something squirted into him. Since it's not the wormer itself that is objectionable, we might train the horse in the following way.

First we will take an old worming syringe. We'll put honey on the outside and let the horse get the honey on his lip. He'll find out that that tastes pretty good. We will repeat this for several days, and then we'll put a little honey in the syringe and squirt it into the horse's mouth. When we go out to ride, or to work with the horse, we'll take him a little treat in the syringe. Moving up from here, to get the texture of the wormer, we will put applesauce in the syringe. We'll repeat this several times.

After a while, when we walk out to the corral with the syringe, our horse will attack us. Soon worming him can be done without a halter because he comes over begging to be wormed.

OVERCOMING FEAR OF FLY SPRAY

It is much harder to get a horse used to being sprayed with a liquid when it's fifteen degrees below zero. For this lesson, pick a nice hot day when the mist would feel good to the horse.

Since we are not supposed to drench the horse in fly spray, and because it is expensive, we will fill the bottle with water for our training.

Put a halter and soft lead on the horse, move him out to the center of the corral or the round pen, and begin spraying. He will move around at first. Don't try to really hang on to him, just direct his movement. Eventually he will learn to stand still and relax. He'll even discover that he likes being sprayed and cooled off.

By following the steps in this chapter, we are now able to pick up our horse's feet, clip and bathe him, worm him, and fly spray him. We can exercise him in open spaces by longeing him, or have him stay put in the same place by ground-tying or hobbling him. The pole exercise helps him with his coordination, which will come in handy as we ride him.

All in all, a horse that has been thoroughly ground trained is a pleasure to be around.

Chapter Ten —————

Improving Our Trail Work

*A*fter we have taken the horse out on a few trail rides, we will want to begin amplifying our training. We'll continue to build control over him, taking care to get the response we are seeking at one level before moving on to the next. At this point, the horse is giving to the bit well. He is navigating around trail obstacles such as trees and brush, goes up and down hills, and will pass fearful objects. He has broken into a trot on his own, and he is learning to slow down and stop on our request. Now it's time for more advanced training.

INTRODUCING THE TROT CUE

While there will be some point during the trail ride where we will want to trot, it is important to wait for the horse to trot on his own the first dozen times or so before trying to introduce a specific trot cue. The reason for this is that we will have to be kicking the horse with our legs to get him to trot, and we really don't want to do this, because he might start bucking.

As the horse becomes more comfortable going into the trot, and as we become more aware that he is going to do it on his own, then we are ready to begin introducing the trot cue.

At this point, our hand, or hands, are held fairly low, inches above the horse's neck and a few inches ahead of the saddle horn.

When the horse begins to go into the trot on his own, we will lift our hands a few inches higher above his neck and move them four to five inches closer to the horse's head. At the same time we will squeeze both legs against his sides. It's important to squeeze, for we don't want to kick him into the trot.

The reason for introducing the trot cue in this manner is that it keeps both the energetic horse, as well as the lazy horse, sensitive to light leg cues. This is accomplished because we are actually asking for the trot at the point that the horse is already going into it.

On a lazy horse, who might want to ignore this cue to trot, we have a tendency to become more aggressive with our legs by kicking him, and in doing so, we actually desensitize the horse. This produces a horse that we refer to as dead sided. We can improve any lazy horse's energy by doing more trotting and loping work on the trail.

As the horse begins to associate the squeezing cue with the trot, it will become easier to get him into this gait. After ten to fifteen times, he will know to go into the trot when we squeeze him with our legs.

TRAINING AT THE TROT

While we're on the trail, we're constantly looking for ways to improve our control over our horse. Once we can get him into the trot, then ninety percent of our trail ride should be done at this gait, with our concentration not on trail riding, but on training. We should constantly be looking for obstacles to ride our horse through, around, or close to, to judge whether or not we are getting the horse to go where we are asking him to go. The reason for training at the trot is that the horse learns quicker, and we can cut down on our training time.

TRAIL EXERCISES

As you are training your horse, realize that there are other exercises that can be done that do not interrupt trail riding. We can be training our horse, and people who are riding with us won't even have to know what we are doing. In fact, we may not want to tell anyone because that ruins the game! We can build from, and on, simple exercises. Here are a few to consider:

1. *Controlling the horse's movement through weight shift:* Riding along the edge of a dirt road, we'll shift in the saddle and put five pounds more pressure on our right foot than on our left. Eventually the horse will walk to the left side of the road. When he gets to the left side of the road, we'll switch and put five pounds of extra pressure in our left stirrup. By doing this exercise, we're not putting any leg pressure on the horse, yet we are teaching him to listen to subtle changes in our weight shifts. If we're feeling really playful, we can announce to our riding companions that "the horse knows his left from his right," as he goes back and forth across the road, while we sit with our hands folded in front of us, reins unattended on his neck.

2. *Giving to the bit:* Riding down the right side of a dirt road, we'll slowly pick up our right rein and ask the horse to drop his head and respond to the bit to the right, without moving his head to the right. In this manner, we are trying to build

softness and responsiveness. We will release as soon as the horse responds and gives to us. We are not trying to pull his head around. What we are trying to do is to give him a cue to move his head. We don't want to pull his head around, or all we'll be proving is that we are stronger than the horse is when he is relaxed, and we're sure not going to be stronger than he is when he's scared or excited. When we pick up on the reins, we don't want to move his head. We want to slowly take the slack out of the reins and let him move it on his own.

3. *Gaining directional control and perfecting our timing:* On a dirt road or a trail, we'll pick out a rock or a bush and try to have the horse pass within two inches of the object. In this way we are again teaching him to go where we want him to go. If the horse fails to pass within six inches of the rock or bush, we need to ask him to make his move earlier. This tells us how our timing is working with the horse. Timing can become pretty important if ten feet too late means we go over a cliff, or that the mare in front of us is going to kick our head off. That's when people learn they have no control over their horse.

   See if you can get the horse to step on a rock or piece of paper. Can you get the horse to take a six-inch shorter step to step on the rock?

4. *Riding specifically:* We can pick out two rocks, two piles of manure, or two flowers, and ask the horse to walk between them. If we miss, we'll know we need to work on our timing. It makes more sense to the horse to walk between bushes on the trail than it does to turn around nothing in an arena. The narrower the path between the two objects, the more specific we are becoming with our horse. We are not asking him to make a turn in a wide-open field, but rather, we are asking him to pass between two specific objects and walk through a narrow twelve-inch opening. That's specific.

5. *Bending the horse around our leg:* We can pick out a single tree, preferably one without a lot of low limbs, and see how close we can get our horse to the trunk. We can also see if we can bend him halfway around the tree. The purpose of this exercise is to see if we can bend the horse around our leg. This will also teach the horse to keep our leg from

bumping into the tree. So as we go halfway around the tree, we will lean to the outside hip, squeezing lightly with our inside leg, pushing the horse's rib cage over as we bring the horse's nose toward the tree. This can be practiced on both sides.

6. *Getting the horse to bend his body with ours:* We can pick out two trees that are close together and teach the horse to flex around the objects. We will be doing the same subtle weight-shifting with our body as we did in exercise five, above. This teaches our horse to do exactly the same thing with his body that we are doing with ours. The horse will soon give this way and then that, weaving in and out among objects. This works for obstacles such as gates and boulders where there is barely enough room to get through. What we are doing is teaching the horse to move with us so that our leg will not be jammed into a rock or gate. This lesson alone is invaluable as we trail ride through cactus and boulders. It's amazing how a horse that doesn't respond to our body in this manner can really bump and bruise us over a hazardous trail, while he comes through unscathed.

7. *Smooth transitions:* We'll pick out a series of objects to ride between, such as two trees, two boulders, or a boulder and a tree, each pair about two feet apart. Before we ride between the first two, we will select the next pair to head for. Prior to riding between the second pair we'll select the third, and so on. In this manner we are working on teaching smooth transitions from the first two objects to the next two. We should have a nice curved line between the objects without having to jerk the horse through, or around, them. This exercise can also be graduated up to the trot and then up to the canter.

These are just some of the exercises you can practice on trail rides. As your horse progresses, you can try trotting him and lifting your seat off the saddle right before asking for the stop. If we do that fifteen times in a trail ride, our horse will stop the minute he feels us leave him. This is like a safety switch on a riding lawn mower and could prevent a lot of accidents.

TEACHING THE FIRST CIRCLE

We all want a nice, responsive horse who doesn't hang on the bit and who moves with us when we ask him to. One important way to get such a horse is to utilize the circle in our training program.

Since any time the horse's ears are in a straight line with his tail he is stiff and unbending, working him in a circle will soften him up and encourage him to bend around our leg.

At this point we have the horse going in and around obstacles. We'll now pick out one object and have him make an even circle around it.

We need in our trail-ride area an open field with an obstacle we can ride around. A pile of manure, a rock, or even a daisy will serve this purpose. We can choose anything specific from which we can easily judge our distance.

We will begin by riding the horse in a circle about twenty feet from the object. Our priorities during this exercise, *in order*, are:

1. To keep the horse from leaning on the bit
2. To keep the horse's nose tipped to the inside of the circle
3. To keep the horse's poll at the elevation we want
4. To keep the horse at an equal distance from the object at every point in the circle and create an arc, or bend, in his body that will be the same as the arc of the circle
5. To keep the horse moving at a constant speed, preferably at the trot

Getting the horse to do the circle properly will take work on our part. This is going to be frustrating, for getting the horse to do just one of the above steps correctly may take a lot of time. We must follow our priorities in sequence. For instance, if the distance from the object is correct, yet the horse's nose is tipped to the outside of the circle, then the horse's body won't be arced, thus the horse will be stiff. This will create problems such as the horse leaning on the bit, or being high headed. We are trying to produce a nice, soft, supple horse, and in order to do that, we need to *follow the sequence.*

While this same exercise can be done in the arena around a plastic cone, it's easier for the rider to keep the horse moving on the trail, and it's also better because the uneven ground will teach the horse to pick up his feet. By doing this exercise out on the trail, the horse also gets a break by being away from home. If we work him in circles in a pen, he may get heavier and heavier on the bit.

There are other things we will want to notice during the circle exercise. If the horse is trying to cut to the inside of the circle, we will squeeze with our inside leg. We will not kick or bump him. Continue holding the horse's head to the inside of the circle. Put light pressure on the outside rein to ask the horse to break at the poll, and continue holding inside-leg pressure until the horse moves off the leg and out to the original diameter of the circle.

If the horse moves too far away from the object we are circling, we will use whatever pressure it takes, and it should take little, on the inside rein to guide the horse back to the original track. Be sure whenever putting pressure on that inside rein that the horse responds by bending his neck, not just by moving his feet.

This process is going to take a couple of hours, including time to let the horse stop and rest occasionally. We are going to have tired legs and our circles are not going to be very even. The horse is going to want to lean on the bit, and we are going to have the tendency to want to hold the horse's head in the circle where we want it. We'll avoid falling into this trap by making sure that we release the horse's head whenever he puts it in the position that we want it in.

As soon as we release him, the horse is going to go straight again. We'll pick up the rein and guide him back to where we want him to hold his head, and then release him again. Remember, you need great patience at this point. What we are trying to teach the horse is that he is to leave his head where we put it, and it's going to take some time for him to learn this lesson. He will improve, though, and he'll get to where he'll leave his head in the position we put it in for longer and longer periods of time.

When we get the horse moving correctly around the object in one direction, we'll repeat the above exercise going the opposite way. This exercise requires a lot of bending and stretching on the horse's part and may create some soreness. He may be a bit stiff the following day until his body becomes accustomed to using its muscles in this manner.

Combine this exercise with those of going around and in between other obstacles that were described earlier in this chapter.

TRAVELING IN A STRAIGHT LINE

Horses do not normally travel in straight lines, so we need an exercise in our training program to teach them how to do this.

We'll begin this exercise out in the open. We don't want to use a road or a trail, because these would support the horse in the direction he is going. We'll pick out two objects that are a considerable distance from us. The objects can be several hundred feet or more apart from each other. With our eye, we'll line them up in a straight line, one behind the other, where we can see only the nearer one of them.

We'll begin trotting toward the first object. When the horse is heading directly at the object, we'll release the reins and any leg contact we may have on him.

With the release of rein and leg pressure, the horse will veer off, either toward the left or toward the right, and we will now be able to see the second object. When this happens, pick up the direct rein, and guide him back over to the straight line we were originally riding. As soon as the horse is lined up again, release the reins until the horse again veers off away from the straight line, and then repeat the process.

Keep practicing this exercise until the horse will continue going in a straight line for longer and longer distances without our having to correct him.

This exercise should be practiced at all three gaits, and at all speeds, as the horse progresses in his training. This will improve all levels of performance, whether on a jumping or a reining horse, for it will teach them not to lean to one side or the other against the reins. This foundation will also become important later on in our training when we do flying lead changes.

CANTERING FOR THE FIRST TIME

We will handle cantering the horse for the first time in much the same way as we approached trotting him for the first time. We will wait for the horse to go from the trot to the canter when it's his idea.

It's important that once the horse goes into the canter, we do not let him build speed too quickly. So the first time he goes into the canter, we will only let him take four or five strides before we bring him back down to a trot and then to a walk. We will reduce his gait by using the turning exercises we did when we first went down from the trot to the walk. The more times we progress in this manner down through the gaits, the more relaxed the horse will become when going into the canter.

Canter cues for correct leads at this point are not taught and are not necessary. Because we have little body control on the horse, trying to get him into a specific lead becomes very difficult for us and for the horse. It's also going to create unwanted problems such as head tossing, the horse's being nervous going into the canter, the horse's elevating his front end, and the horse's becoming confused.

BACKING FOR THE FIRST TIME

In order for the horse to back correctly, he needs to be able to give to the bit and to drop his head when we pick up on the reins. He also needs to be able to flex, or bend, at the poll, and he needs to be able to go into the trot on cue.

In asking him to take the first few steps back, we need to ask the horse to give his head to the right, or to the left.

Pick up on the outside rein and ask him to flex at the poll, and wait. The horse will begin to shift his weight backward. As soon as this happens, release his head and pet him. Keep repeating this process until he'll take a step backward. If he begins to move forward, gradually alternate the pressure from one rein to the other until he stops his forward movement.

Basically what we are doing is bending the horse's head off in one direction, say to the right. As soon as he gives his head to the right, we're releasing the pressure.

If the horse begins to move forward, we'll increase the pressure. As soon as he stops his forward movement, we'll release some of the pressure but continue to apply enough to maintain his bending to one side and flexing at the poll. We also need to use our body to tell the horse we want him to back up, so at this point, we will shift our weight back slightly in the saddle as we lightly squeeze with our legs right behind the horse's elbows. Remember, our leg pressure means for the horse to move. The reins don't have anything to do with speed, so pulling on them will not move the horse.

As we ask the horse to back, it is important that we mentally visualize the horse backing. We need to accept a few backward steps at first, before asking for more. However, backing distances of ten to twelve steps should not take very long to accomplish. Speed and the horse's backing in a straight line are not important at this stage. The most important thing is that as the horse backs up, there be no pressure or pull on the bit or on the reins.

After backing, wait a couple of seconds before asking the horse to move forward.

CROSSING OBSTACLES

While riding out on the trail there will be times when we will want to cross streams, logs, bridges, and other such obstacles. The training method for crossing any of these objects is the same. We will describe it here for crossing water.

I consider people who fight their horses each time to cross a running creek, to be a lot more patient than I am. I want to overcome the horse's fear of water crossing as quickly as possible so I don't ever have to go through it again in the horse's life.

In order for the horse to learn this lesson, he cannot be scared. It would be hard for anyone who is afraid of water to concentrate on crossing a rushing creek if someone was hitting him with a buggy whip to make him hurry. So beating and spurring a frightened animal will only justify his fear. If we want the horse to cross an obstacle calmly, then we must have him calm for most, if not all, of the time. This calmness is a prerequisite in order for him to learn that the obstacle will not hurt him.

What I've learned from the following system is that, by using it, I will actually have the horse through the creek *quicker* than with any other method I've tried. This doesn't take any longer than beating the horse across. It's faster and safer, and after we've completed the lesson, we won't have a problem next time.

First we need to set our goals. If our goal is to just get the horse across the creek, we can get out the bulldozer and pull him across. This isn't a whole lot different from people dragging a horse across with another horse, by crossing another horse first and coaxing the reluctant one across, or by getting off the horse and getting in the water and playing to encourage his participation in water sports.

Our goal will be to get the horse across the creek at a calm, consistent walk so the next time we approach water we don't have to go through the same thing.

During this exercise our horse's feet will either be at the stop, or at the walk, and we'll keep in mind our three rules for training. Remember, the technique must be safe for us. It must be safe for the horse. And finally, the horse must be calmer after the lesson than before it started. Keeping these three rules in mind throughout this lesson will help us to control our impatience.

If we make a general request, we're going to get a general response, so we'll be specific. We will pick a six-inch spot on the creek from which to cross, and we'll work on getting the horse to face that specific spot the whole time. The six-inch spot can be anywhere on the creek, as long as it is on the same side we're crossing from.

If you're more comfortable, you can get off your horse and walk up to the creek to pick your spot, but do not get off the horse to walk him across the water. I've been stepped on too many times to consider that a safe crossing method.

Once our spot is selected, we *will not change it,* even if when we get close to the water we discover it's not the perfect place to cross. We're being specific. The horse knows it. If we change our mind, we're giving the horse the right to second guess us, thereby telling him it's OK if *he* picks the spot. It isn't. We don't want him to pick the spot, we want to do it.

The reins will control the horse's nose, where he looks. Keep his nose facing the spot by using a direct rein on him. This is what you want to do even if you are riding an advanced horse.

Keep the horse's nose facing the spot you have selected by using a direct rein on him, even if he is an advanced horse.

Again, our legs do not signal move forward, they only request movement. When we squeeze or kick and the horse moves, this means we cannot squeeze him again until he stops moving, because he's doing what we asked him to do. If we're riding a green horse we will not have leg cues to use on him at this point.

Like everything else in our training, it's important that we listen to the horse. He'll tell us what we can and cannot do. As the horse walks up to the creek, he'll stop. The horse is now telling us where we're going to start our training.

A horse may hesitate forty feet from the water, but if he's well trained he'll go to within thirty feet. Already he's a little nervous, and there's more pressure on him because he's not ready to be there.

A lot of horses and riders start out knowing they'll have a problem at the creek. The horse says "I don't want to," and the rider says "Oh yes you will." At this point there may not be any visible quarreling going on. There's no big rear-up, no heavy kicking, and the horse isn't backing up. But what has happened is that the rider has kicked the horse up to the obstacle, and the horse is nervous about being there.

If the horse is uncomfortable at thirty feet, we'll take him back to forty to begin the lesson, since his concern tells us we were wrong in moving him closer.

We'll let him stand at his comfort point until he's completely relaxed. The longer we wait here, the better it is, because if we take him closer and he gets excited, he'll know he can return to this spot and relax.

When the horse is completely comfortable and we think we can get away with it, we'll give him the cue to move by squeezing him with our legs. However far the horse moves forward before he stops, pet him. That's his reward for doing what we've asked. Stand with the horse relaxed to the point where he's almost bored before asking him to move again. Remember, the horse must be completely calm before we move on to the next step. That's the secret to this lesson. We will continue this slow and easy pace until we are a foot away from the creek with the horse calm and relaxed the entire time.

If during this series of moves the horse steps backward, relax. When he's backing up there's nothing we can do with our reins or legs that will be right. We have to sit and wait for him to stop. He's already excited and frightened, and his body is in a prime position

Let the horse relax at each point so he will know that if you take him closer to the stream and he gets excited, he can return here and relax.

to rear. Relax and leave the animal alone as long as he is looking at that six-inch spot. He does not have to face the creek head-on. His body can be parallel to the water as long as his nose is aimed at the creek.

A friend passed along to me some wise advice his grandfather had given him years ago when they were working cattle. My friend had been concerned that the cattle would get away from him.

"Grandson," the wise man said, "just wait. The United States is surrounded by water on three sides. If we watch the Canadian border, your cattle won't get away."

The same is true here. Wait. Remember, this has nothing to do with patience and everything to do with staying alive.

When the horse stops backing, wait for him to relax. This can take anywhere from ten seconds to two minutes. When he's relaxed, and we think we can give him the cue to move forward, we do so. Again, any direction he moves in is all right. We'll relax the pressure of our legs against him once he moves, and all we'll concentrate on at this point is for him to look at the creek.

The narrower the span of water, the harder it will be to get the horse to put his feet in it. If we're crossing a creek the size of a garden hose, this means that we've got a lot of work to do to get his feet where we want them.

If the horse walks toward the creek, pet him. He'll probably turn to the right, or to the left, or begin backing up, but as long as his feet are moving, we don't tell him he is going in the wrong direction.

Eventually the horse will stop. Then we'll repeat the procedure to get him to approach the creek. After two or three times, the horse may be next to the creek or ten feet away. At this point, we'll probably be close to our six-inch spot. Horses can cross water at pretty steep places, so don't worry if your spot doesn't look as good up close as it did far away. Repeat the procedure until your horse is right next to the creek.

Again, listen to the horse. If he's nervous, or rearing or misbehaving at the water, then we've overexposed him. We need to take him back to a point where we can set up the condition and get the response we want. The only time we're in physical danger with a horse is when we've overexposed him and lost his attention.

Let the horse stand at the water's edge a long time, three to four minutes. We might even want to look at our watch, because most of us think ten seconds is a long time. We can stay at the creek as long as we like as long as we are not in any danger.

Standing there, we will have some slack in the reins, for we cannot hold the horse's head all the time. Have enough slack so that the horse can lower his head to reach the water. When he does explore the water, he may snort and suck (lean back) from it. Don't pull on his mouth, for you'll be telling him there's a problem. The biggest mistake we can make here is to bump the horse with the bit. Remember, any time you give your horse the slightest bump, he's saying *"What? What?"* The effect on him is similar to the effect on you of hearing your dentist saying "Whoops!" when he's doing a root canal.

Keep enough slack in the reins so the horse can lower his head to reach the water.

I once went to a doctor for a problem I had with my thumb. As he worked on me, I noticed he had his hand out and was examining his own thumb while working on mine.

"Hmmm," he mused, "let's see, there are supposed to be two tendons here." He wiggled his thumb. "Yes, yes, that's right."

That's right? Tell me, where's my confidence now? Don't bump the bit when the horse is examining the water.

If the horse decides he doesn't like the creek and turns away, say to the right, bring him all the way back the way he came. Do not make a circle. Even if he goes 270 degrees, bring him back the same way he came when he was trying to escape. Do not turn all the way around and approach the creek again. This way, he's traveling in the same direction over the same road. He'll see the same scenery, and he's not getting a vacation. He's gained nothing. This is a mental game. If you let him go all the way around, he gets a mental break, relief. Returning him the same direction will also maintain his concentration on the spot at which we're trying to cross.

If the creek is less than ten feet wide, the horse is going to jump it the first time. This is where the biggest wreck of this lesson is likely to occur, so be sure to hang on for the jump. After his leap, let him go thirty or forty yards, which is his reward for crossing the creek. Then turn him around to cross back over, and after his second jump across, give him only a twenty-yard reward.

He'll jump the creek maybe ten or fifteen times. Each time, shorten the reward time before you turn him around and ask him to recross.

Jumping across water is not only not fun, it can be dangerous. It can also be irritating to the horse in front of you that you're landing on.

Once the horse has become comfortable jumping the creek, our next goal will be to get him to step into it. On his next jump, we will catch him with the bit while he is in midair. Do not pull straight back on the bit, but turn him up or down the creek. Surprise! He's now got all four feet in the water. Take him up the creek fifteen steps or so and let him play. Take him out of the creek. Go up the creek twenty yards, and cross. Now down the creek twenty yards, crossing at two or three different places. We'll do this twenty or more times successfully, before we're done.

Never kick the horse across the water, or across any obstacle.

The same system used in crossing water can be applied to everything we want to cross. If we're teaching the horse to cross a trail-course bridge, we'll pick a spot in the center of the bridge for the horse's nose to face. Since this is a training bridge, on the ground and without water under it, we can choose the direction in which to cross it. The first few times we cross, the horse's front feet may be on the bridge while one or both back feet may be off it. Once the front feet are consistent, we'll work on the back. Again, as in the water crossing, we'll break the exercise down into steps as we work toward our goal.

If we're crossing a tarp or a piece of plastic, we'll pick an eyelet or some such point on the object and direct the horse's nose to it. On a log, we will again pick a spot and aim the horse's nose at it.

This is where my lack of patience pays off. If the whole process of training my horse to cross water has taken twenty minutes, the odds are good that the next time we'll do it in a minute or less.

That's progress.

Chapter Eleven ━━━━━━

Advancing the
Trail Work

I f we have followed the training program to this point, we
have a horse that we can ride down the trail, one that will
walk, trot, and canter, as well as back up and cross
obstacles. Now it's time to improve on our horse's response and to
ask more of him.

The neat thing about training horses is that we can start over
every day. We're all going to make mistakes, but the horse is like a
giant blackboard that we can erase and start over. Our horse can
be fifteen years old, but if we decide we want to change
something, we can.

THE HORSE'S SENSITIVITY, OR WHAT WE SETTLE FOR

Understanding how sensitive a horse is helps us to know how much or how little (leg pressure, weight shift, etc.) we need when we cue him. If a horse can't feel anything less than two pounds of pressure on the reins, then we can't give one pound of pressure and expect him to respond. The ideas that a horse is tough mouthed, or cannot feel a cue are untrue.

Similarly, all horses are capable of feeling the slightest shift of weight or movement on their backs. Recognizing the point at which the horse can distinguish whether or not we've moved on his back, determines how light our cues can be.

Remember that little eight-year-old girl who had grown up with her horse and could whip the socks off the pros in the show ring? Now she's seventeen, and that horse can do anything and everything that that girl asks him to do. Teach him something new? No problem. It's done in a matter of minutes. The girl, because she's had such great success with her horse, wants to go out and train horses. She quickly discovers that it's harder work than she had anticipated. These horses aren't as bright as her own! The reason they don't seem as bright is simply because she and her horse are so in tune with each other, and her horse is so accustomed to her idiosyncrasies and what her movements mean that he can pick up much more readily what she's explaining to him than can a strange horse.

We are instinctual creatures. If we begin to walk forward, our upper bodies—that is our heads, shoulders, and arms—move first in preparation for the movement of our feet and legs. These are subconscious motions, and we make them in the saddle as well, whether we are asking the horse to move forward, or backward, or turning right or left. If we realize that the horse can feel these movements, then the subconscious movements themselves can become the horse's cues, and he will automatically respond to them.

If we are thinking about asking our horse to move back, our body is going to shift to a backing position without our consciously putting it there. The horse can feel this subconscious movement, and this will become the cue that we will eventually want him to back on. Our thought plus our subconscious movement translate into the horse's backward movement. No pulling on the reins, no kicking, just a thought, and back.

HAND MOVEMENT

Before we can get the horse to respond to our thoughts (or silent cues), we need to work on our hand movement. If you ride with one hand, say your left, place it a few inches above the saddle horn, keeping slack in your reins. If you ride with two hands, they will both be on the reins. This position is going to mean "back" to the horse. Now move your hand four inches ahead of the saddle horn. This position is going to mean "stop." Moving four inches ahead of the stop position will mean "forward."

It is important to understand that our hand position does not signal "move" to the horse, it only tells him in which direction to move, in this case, forward (eight inches ahead of the saddle horn), stop (four inches forward), and back (just ahead and above of the saddle horn). We use our legs to tell the horse to move. So if our legs are telling the horse to move, and our hands are telling him in which direction to move, we should be able to control both the movement of the horse and the direction he takes.

This is a really hard concept to learn and to practice if you are used to guiding or feeling pressure on the reins, or on the bit, with your hands. It's going to take a lot of concentration to let it go and to break old habits. Remember, reins communicate direction; legs communicate movement.

TEACHING THE STOP

The stop will be taught at the walk. With some horses, this is an easy thing to teach; others have more energy and don't want to waste time by stopping.

First we'll get the horse to hesitate, to slow his steps, rather than actually stop. We'll get him to pause for a second and then let him continue walking. This is a good beginning, especially if you are working with a horse who is unwilling to stand still. From this point, we will build to a longer hesitation.

Pulling straight back with both reins, using a snaffle bit will have little effect on stopping a thousand-pound animal. So as we teach the stop, we will not pull back on both reins simultaneously, but will work first one, then the other. Also since the snaffle does not give us much leverage, we will need to get the horse out of a straight line and not have his ears in line with his tail.

With the horse walking, we'll begin by picking up the reins. We'll break the straight line by keeping the horse's nose tipped one to four inches off to the right (using the right rein in the same manner as when we taught the horse to give to the bit), and then we'll pick up on the left rein. The right rein keeps the horse soft; the left, in this case, will cause a change in direction. This will cause the horse to hesitate, or pause, in midstep. This is the beginning of the stop. If you use verbal cues, you can ask the horse to "whoa" as you pick up on the left rein and he pauses as he positions his feet to change direction. We will build from this first hesitation to a longer pause, to a stop of one second, then a stop of two seconds, to ten, and so on.

Once the horse is stopping for longer periods of time, we can progress further. Trail riding can be the easiest thing a horse can do, or it can be one of the most advanced things he can do. We can help teach the stop to the horse by riding in front of other horses. Since the horse wants to slow down and stay with his pals, we are likely to find him more responsive to our stop request. In this position, we also have the opportunity to teach the horse to go forward.

It is harder to teach a horse to stop when he is in the rear of the pack, because he is eager to stay with the herd. Frequently, if we start this lesson from this position, we'll find ourselves in a push/pull contest.

After the horse is performing well in the front of the pack, then let the other horses get closer and closer to catching up with him. Advance from that to having him even with the other horses. Then advance to having the horse wait a second or two behind them. Keep building until, when the horse is even with the other horses, he will stop when asked and will then walk quickly up to them. Build on these stops until the horse will stop, even though he is farther and farther away from his friends. Remember, if, for example, the horse won't stop five feet behind the pack for five seconds, go back to, say, having him stop three feet behind them for two seconds, and then build from there.

RIDING FIGURE EIGHTS

Once the horse is capable of doing single circles consistently while moving at a constant speed, with the proper poll elevation, and giving to the bit correctly, then we can progress to figure eights with a change of direction in between the circles. Riding figure eights will begin to teach the horse to neck rein.

For this exercise I like to pick out two objects, which can be trees or rocks or the like, that are about thirty to forty feet apart. We need this distance so that we can ride in approximately fifteen- to twenty-foot circles. We want to concentrate our attention on the horse's nose as he changes direction from one circle to the other. We're seeking a smooth transition, where the horse's nose does not straighten out or drift to the outside of the circle, his poll does not elevate, and he does not jerk his head as he changes direction from one circle to the other. As the horse does the circle, his ears should not be in line with his tail. If they are, we are building in stiffness and resistance.

As we prepare to make the change from one circle to the other, we must insure that the horse is relaxed, and that his body is in a correct position. This means that the horse is relaxed and not leaning on the bit, his nose is tipped slightly to the inside of the circle, his poll is at the elevation we request, he is at an equal distance from the object at every point in the circle, creating an arc or bend in his body that is the same as the arc of the circle, and he is moving at a constant trot speed. If you've picked a spot to make the change of circles, and the horse is out of position to make a nice, smooth change of direction, then forget the change and continue on in the direction you are already going until he is in the proper position.

Eventually what we are going to do is to offset the two circles. We will have one circle, then a straight line off that circle and then a circle in the opposite direction. The pattern will look like this:

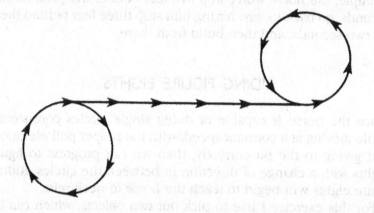

As we go into the straight line, we want the horse's body to straighten out. Now his ears will be in line with his tail, his head will be at the correct elevation, his nose will have popped, or straightened, out, and he will be breaking at the poll. The longer the horse stays in the correct position, the farther we will go in the straight line.

The horse isn't going to stay perfect forever, so if the elevation of his head or his nose position changes, that is when we have to start the other circle, to the left if we were traveling right before. Whenever the horse is in the wrong position, we can get him in the correct position by taking him in a circle.

As the horse improves at making a simple change of direction in a thirty-foot circle or figure eight at the trot, then we can improve his skills by increasing the speed of the trot and by shrinking the size of the circle. A horse needs to be more responsive to make a change of direction in a fifteen-foot circle than he does in a thirty-foot circle. His change will obviously also have to be quicker.

It's important that the horse, during the change of direction, does not lean his body to the right or to the left. We want to be careful as we are riding not to lean our own bodies too much to the inside as we ask the horse to make his changes. Doing so will cause him to begin dropping a shoulder, which could become a habit. A dropped shoulder will cause problems later during the flying lead change, which we will discuss in Chapter Thirteen.

THE HEAD SET

There are times when we will want to place our horse's head in a specific position. The position we set the head in may not always be the same. For instance we may want it in one position for one class and another for yet another class.

I've found that ties-downs and martingales, either running or German, do not work consistently for head setting. The problem with these gimmicks is that the horse knows the minute that they are removed.

By using the principle of releasing the horse whenever his head is in the correct position, we are able to move the horse's poll to any position we want by changing our release point. The breed of horse or the riding style does not matter, because this principle will work the same with any breed or style.

The better our horse gets at finding the release points, the quicker we can move or readjust his head's position. With this type of training, we now have a way to ask for different poll positions.

If we are riding a high-headed horse, we need to fully understand the working application of both the full-cheek and the D-ring snaffle bits. If we use these bits as they were designed, they can help us effectively retrain the high-headed horse.

The natural tendency for us, as well as for our horse, is to resist pressure. This explains why our horse pulls against us when we pull on the reins. In order to teach him the correct response, we must first understand why he will want to change. He will want relief from our pulling on the bit in his mouth.

So first we must decide the level at which we want his head held, and then we must release the reins when he does what we've asked. Although initially, the horse will comply for release, he will eventually get lighter and lighter on less and less pressure from us, if we are consistent in our timing of when to pull on the reins and when to release them.

Basically, the horse has a 100-degree vertical range of motion with his head. He can put his nose on the ground or lift it as high as he can. If we decide that we want the horse's poll at between 40 and 50 degrees, then we must hold pressure on the reins whenever the horse's head is not in this position. We will only release him when he places his head in the correct range.

Although our goal is to have the horse's head at 40–50 degrees, we cannot begin there. We will start with where the horse holds his head naturally, and build from there.

To begin our training, let's say the horse is holding his head at 85 degrees. As we add pressure to the reins, the horse looks for relief and takes his head up to 88 degrees, but we continue to hold the pressure. Since that didn't relieve him, he starts to drop his head, and when it gets to 85 degrees, we release the pressure and pet him.

We will repeat this process until the horse drops his head to 82 degrees, and then we'll release and pet him again.

The horse learns that if he drops his head when we pick up the reins, we'll release him, giving him the relief he is seeking. Most people don't know why they pull on the horse. The saying "High hands, high horse" is a bunch of garbage. Only not releasing the horse creates high headedness.

We will continue in this manner until the horse is carrying his head in the 40–50 degree range. A table for explaining this concept would be:

100 Degrees	Highest Point
90 Degrees	Pressure on Reins
80 Degrees	Pressure on Reins
70 Degrees	Pressure on Reins
60 Degrees	Pressure on Reins
51 Degrees	Pressure on Reins
50 Degrees	Release Reins
40 Degrees	Release Reins
39 Degrees	Pressure on Reins
20 Degrees	Pressure on Reins
10 Degrees	Pressure on Reins
0–9 Degrees	Lowest Point

This principle will also work for the horse who holds his head too low. In this case, we will apply pressure on the reins when the horse's head is lower than we would like. If the horse drops his head even lower, we will maintain the pressure. Once he raises his head a degree or two, we will release the pressure. We will continue building on this, step by step, until his head is in the correct position.

Using this exercise we can set our horse's head in any position without the use of any gimmicks.

Chapter Twelve ____

Beginning
Arena Work

T here are a number of exercises that can be practiced in the arena. These are convenient for the days when a trainer does not have the time to take the horse out on a trail ride, or just wants to work on a specific exercise or set of exercises.

CONE EXERCISES

Setting cones or markers in an arena gives the trainer an opportunity to practice a wide variety of specific riding patterns without having to get off the horse and move the cones around. These exercises will help both the beginning horse and the most advanced performer. Used as a general warm-up routine for everyday use, they promote good habits in both the horse and the rider.

The cones allow the rider to ride over a very narrow path while concentrating on keeping the horse's head, neck, and body in the correct position.

It is important that we keep in mind while we are riding these patterns, that we have a priority list of things we want from our horse. They are:

1. The horse's nose must be tipped to the inside of the turn.

2. The horse's poll should be at the desired height.

3. The horse is on the vertical and is soft in our hands, and his neck is relaxed as he is responding to us. There should be no pressure on the direct, or inside, rein.

4. The horse should have an arc in his body equal to the arc of the circle we are riding. Here we can use our inside leg (the leg closest to the hub of the circle) to round out the horse's body, or to push his shoulders over to the outside of the circle. This encouragement with the inside leg can also be used if the horse wants to fall into the center of the circle.

5. The horse should stay on the track and go where we are asking him to go. He will keep the same distance from the cones at all points, and make all changes of direction smooth with nice arcs, not angles.

6. The horse's speed should remain constant. We have chosen the speed we want—walk, slow trot, fast trot, or canter—and we want him to keep it constant. The slow trot is what I like to use the most, with a bit of fast trotting thrown in. Cantering is done, but only on a more finished horse. If we do this exercise at the canter, on a green horse, we may find ourselves practicing mistakes.

7. As the horse changes from one direction to the other, his head should not raise, nor should his nose pop out forward.

His head should swing smoothly and easily in one clean sweep from one circle to the other.

These exercises fill a niche in our training program. Many times it is much easier to go out on a nice, long trail ride rather than practice specific riding patterns such as these, which are often boring and hard to concentrate on. However, the results in respect to your horse's performance level are well worth it. If you only have twenty minutes to practice these patterns before you go out on that ride, you'll still find a great benefit for you and your horse.

For the following exercises, three cones should be set up to form a triangle, about sixty feet on a side.

FIFTEEN-FOOT CIRCLES

Ride circles approximately fifteen feet in diameter until the horse is doing well. Repeat in both directions.

FIGURE EIGHTS

Ride large circles approximately thirty feet in diameter. When the horse is doing well in both directions, begin making figure eights.

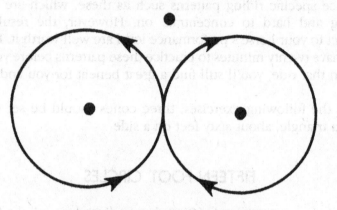

SHRINKING FIGURE EIGHTS

Ride larger figure eights around top cones. When the horse is doing well here, make smooth transitions to smaller figure eights from the top to the bottom cone.

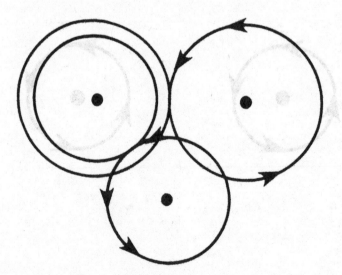

INSIDE CIRCLES

Inside the cones, make three small circles or figure eights in changing directions. Come as close to the cones as possible and keep the circles even. Transitions should be smooth.

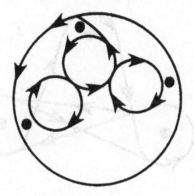

CIRCLES AND EIGHTS

Make a large circle on the inside of the cones, about sixty feet in diameter. When a smooth change is possible, switch to two smaller figure eights around the base cones.

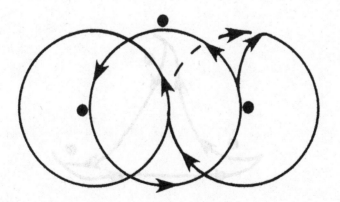

CIRCLES AND STRAIGHT LINES

This exercise has small (eight-foot) half circles around cones and straight lines between the cones. Be careful the horse's head does not come up and his nose out.

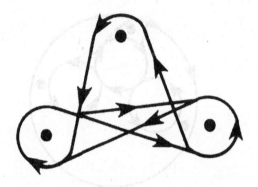

ROLLBACKS

While this exercise is beneficial to any horse, it will particularly help improve the horse who is not working well off his hindquarters. Make half or quarter circles around the cone, and then roll the horse back toward the cone. The half circle helps put the horse's body in the right position to make the rollback easier for him to do.

CIRCLES AND LINES AGAIN

This exercise incorporates smooth circles and straight lines. While it is a relaxing exercise, it also needs the rider's close attention to the horse's nose and head positions.

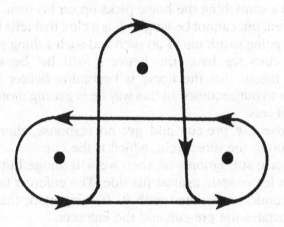

TEACHING A HORSE TO RATE HIS SPEED

We all know that a horse has different walk, trot, and canter speeds. When a horse comes shuffling in for his dinner he may be at a slow trot. If something startles him, his trot speed will increase. And so it goes through all of a horse's gaits.

Rating speed means that we are asking the horse to go either faster or slower in a specific gait. If a horse can trot at twenty miles per hour and we can only get him to trot at fifteen miles per hour, we have already lost twenty-five percent of the horse's potential.

The bigger the difference we can get between a horse's high and low speeds, the more speed control we'll have over him. We'll also end up with a ten-speed model partner, instead of a three-speed model.

The round pen provides us with a controlled training environment where we will be safe in teaching this lesson. In the round pen, the horse can't run away with us, and since there are no corners, he will run more smoothly.

In training our horses, we need to understand that we have pre-cues, cues, and enforcers. It's also important that we keep this order when training. As an example, if I am reining my horse to the right and I first lay the rein against his neck, that is a pre-cue. Because it's something the horse picks up on his own, a pre-cue can be given, but cannot be taught. It is a clue that tells the horse, "Oh, he's going to ask me to do such and such a thing next." The more pre-cues we have, the better it will be, because their existence means that the horse is becoming lighter and more responsive to our requests. In this way he is getting more chances to work off less.

If we give the pre-cue and get no response, then we will continue on to the direct rein, which is the cue.

If the horse still ignores us, then we will nudge him with the enforcer, a leg or spur, against his side. The enforcer usually has some discomfort associated with it. It's important that the cue always separates the pre-cue and the enforcer.

Enforcers should never be used as cues or the horse will eventually stop what it is that we are asking him to do. For example, if we kick the horse to get him to trot, and if we continue kicking him while he is trotting, he won't like it and will quit doing the thing (trotting) that causes him to be uncomfortable.

To teach our horse to rate his speed, we will first need a cue that tells him, "Go as fast as you can in this gait." This cue will be the same for the walk, the trot, and the canter.

We will start this lesson at the trot. Our pre-cues will be: (1) raising our hands forward, away from the saddle horn, (2) standing up in the saddle and leaning forward, and (3) kissing to the horse. If the horse doesn't respond to these pre-cues by increasing his speed, we will move on to the cue.

The cue will be first a light squeeze with both legs. If this doesn't work, we will move on to bumping the horse with both legs.

Finally, if the horse is not trotting fast, we'll call in the enforcer. This will be a hard kick with both spurs, which will cause the horse to jump out.

The hardest part of rating speed is to learn the patience to go through the entire process, step by step. As we work the horse in the round pen, he may want to cut across it, or he may want to change directions. Don't worry about this, just ask him to keep moving. Speed will take the horse to the outside of the round pen. Be patient, for it might take fifteen minutes to get the horse going consistently in one direction. Do not pull on the reins.

Once the horse has learned this sequence he needs to learn a cue that tells him, "Go as slow as you can in this gait."

Since the horse can feel a big difference between trotting at a rate of two miles per hour and at nine miles per hour, we are going to teach him a cue that will tell him "Now you are going to go as slow as you can while maintaining the trot."

Regardless of whether we are increasing or decreasing the horse's speed, it's important that he does not break his gait.

Remember the game from the first part of the book where the horse says, "You have to pull on my mouth to slow me down, and if you do, I win?" Well, we now have to figure out a way to slow this horse down without getting into his mouth.

Our pre-cues will be: (1) moving our hands back to where they are even with the saddle horn, with slack in the reins, and (2) sitting back down on the saddle.

Our cue will be to relax in the saddle. If this does not slow the horse down, we will begin to bounce in the saddle to get his attention, and finally, we will pick up on the reins. There will be no enforcer for this cue.

Why will the horse want to slow down? First, if we bounce in the saddle, it's going to hurt him. Also, since we're pushing him around the pen as fast as he can go, he may be tired. The longer we wait before offering him the opportunity to slow down, the better our chances will be that he will take it.

After trotting him fast for at least five minutes, give the pre-cues: hands back and sitting down. If nothing happens, relax in the saddle, count two seconds, and begin bouncing.

The horse will not stop, but will look back at you as he notices the change you have made. His ears may be back a bit, his head may be up, and his speed will be the same. Go around the pen two or three times before standing back up and giving the cue to "Go as fast as you can in this gait." Repeat this three or four times.

If, the next time you offer the chance to slow down, the horse has still not caught on, pick up on the reins.

Once we notice the requested change in the gait, we should relax. Now that the horse is starting to understand these cues and we're getting results, we can improve on what we've got. In all of our training, it is much harder to get results than it is to tune up those results. For instance, once the horse backs three feet, it's easier to teach him to back ten feet than it was to teach that first backward step.

In teaching a horse to rate his speed, we can see a major difference in two hours. Be sure to watch your horse to insure you are not stressing him. If he's hot and tired, leave the lesson and continue it another day.

At the canter, any holes in the process will be tripled or quadrupled; at the walk, the holes will shrink. Work on this lesson, from an extended trot to a slow, almost in place trot, off and on over a couple of weeks.

THE TIPOVER POINT

When we roll a horse back against a fence, there is a lot more to it than just running him into the barrier and jerking him around to get him to turn. Rolling a horse back accustoms him to working off his hindquarters.

There is a tipover point, or rollover point, that we can use to our advantage. This is a spot we pick on the fence where, if the horse's nose comes near it and we release him, his body is committed to continuing on through a turn, or rollback.

This lesson will be taught at the fast trot in the round pen. For this exercise, our hands need to move as though they are in slow motion. When we make our request and release the horse as he makes the turn, he should come out of it at the trot. He should be moving at all times.

If he comes out of the turn at the canter, let him go for a few strides and then slow him down.

If I am riding the horse and I release him too early, he will straighten up and move forward, without turning. If I release him too late, he will become heavier on the bit. So it's important to release the reins at the point where the horse is already committed to making his turn.

A horse that gets used to using lots of energy through his turns will, when we ask him to stop, stop light, not heavy.

We will also use the tipover point when we are teaching leads, and also if we are working with a horse that is one-sided.

As we practice this exercise, we will find that it will take less and less pressure on the reins as the horse begins to respond to our request for a rollback.

Chapter Thirteen ━━━━

Leads and Cues

B efore we begin to teach leads to the horse he should perform all the exercises around the triangle cones, without mistakes. This prerequisite will eliminate as many "practiced" mistakes as possible. Since the horse doesn't know what a mistake is, when he makes one, he will be thinking he is doing what we want him to do, and he will be inclined to repeat, or "practice," the mistake. So it's much easier not to practice mistakes in the first place, by always making sure that the horse is ready before we move him on to the next area of training.

Horses vary greatly in the ease with which they pick up their leads. There are several training techniques available to us, depending upon the degree of difficulty involved in teaching a particular horse.

In deciding which method to use, it's important that the technique we select will not cause us problems later on. Popping into the lead, tail wringing, and rushing through a flying lead change are generally caused by the method used early in the horse's training.

It is also important that we don't assume that a horse is going to be difficult, when, in fact, he may easily learn to take his leads correctly.

Our first clue as to whether or not the horse will pick up his lead correctly comes when we are trotting him in circles. While we are in a fast trot in our circle, we'll do nothing more than encourage the horse to pick up his speed. We'll do this by using verbal commands, standing up in the stirrups, and using the other techniques outlined in the rating speed lesson.

We want to make going into the canter as comfortable as possible for the horse. At this point, all we are trying to do is to get him into the canter to see if he will naturally pick up the correct lead. If he goes into the canter correctly, on the right lead, then we'll let him lope a few circles. Since we want the canter to be relaxing to the horse, we should not be doing too much correction at this point. Later, we'll correct a gait that's too fast or too slow. For now, we want him relaxed and loping.

CUES FOR LEADS

As our horse gets better at going from the fast trot into the lope on the correct lead, we'll begin establishing the specific cue we want for the canter on that lead. For example, when we are asking for the right lead, and our cue for that lead is squeezing with our left leg, then just before we think he's going to make the transition from the trot to the canter, we'll slowly squeeze our left leg against him. We want to always squeeze our leg against the horse very slowly. Kicking him will only cause an overreaction. Introducing the lead in this manner is very easy on the horse and causes no bad habits. We are setting up the condition, our leg squeezing on the left side, and the horse is responding by picking up the correct lead, leading with his right leg. If we do this often enough it will become automatic to the horse.

It would be nice if this was all it took for every horse, but, unfortunately, that's just not the case. So the "what if's" begin here.

We'll start working in a circle to the right. Once the horse is in a fast trot, we'll slowly squeeze our left leg against him (asking for the right lead). If the horse does not go on the correct lead, then very slowly pick up the outside rein and gradually add pressure until he breaks from the canter back to the trot. Once he is back in the trot, repeat the above process again. Go through it at least ten times to see if the horse is going to pick up the lead. If not, then on the eleventh time, just before he goes into the canter, add just a little pressure to the outside rein. You must still encourage the horse to go faster. Sometimes this will be all it takes to get him to pick up the lead, but if not, go to the next step.

Take your horse to the round pen. Repeat the above sequence, beginning with *not* touching the outside rein at all and progressing to picking it up and adding a little pressure. If the horse still does not pick up the correct lead, then proceed to the following.

Let's say the horse is having trouble with his left lead. Begin by trotting him around the round pen to the right or clockwise. Ask the horse to turn left toward the fence and ask him to hurry. Don't jerk on the reins to make him turn fast, use your legs. Remember, the reins only tell the horse which direction to go, our legs tell him to move.

Keep your hand speed slow and consistent. As the horse goes into the turn, squeeze or kick him to hurry as he comes out of the turn. What he should do is to canter out of the turn on the correct (left) lead. If the horse wants to slow down, we'll keep encouraging him with our legs. It doesn't matter at this point if he comes out of the turn too fast, we can work on slowing him down later, after he's taking his leads correctly.

Now we have the horse on the left lead, cantering counter-clockwise around the pen. Slowly pick up the outside rein and add pressure until he drops back to a fast trot. Trot a few more times around the pen and then ask for the turn in to the fence to the right. Ask him to hurry out of the turn in the same manner as before. Again, he will come out on the correct lead, only this time it will be on the right lead instead of the left.

When the horse comes out on the correct lead, let him travel on it at least three or four trips around the pen so he becomes more familiar and comfortable with traveling on that lead.

If he does not come out on the correct lead, you asked for speed too late when coming out of the turn, and he trotted out, instead of loping out, when he completed his turn. In this case, turn him back the other direction as quickly as possible and start over again. At this point, we do not want him loping around the pen on the incorrect lead.

This system works with ninety-five percent of the horses who do not want to take the correct lead. The other five percent I take into a square pen about forty feet on a side for further training.

Here's what to do in the square pen. Begin by trotting the horse to the right. Leave the reins down and loose, unless the horse begins to cut in toward the center of the pen. If he cuts in, pull the outside rein to get him back on the fence. Ask the horse to trot and then go into the canter. The horse is not going to want to canter, because it's difficult for him in such close quarters.

The horse will want to cut in. Keep pressure on him to canter as you direct him into the corners. It is very difficult for the horse to go close to the corner at the canter in the wrong lead. This system will work on the most difficult lead problems. Remember though, you're going to have to push very hard here to get your horse to canter. After doing this exercise a few times, the horse will begin picking up that difficult lead. He will not wring his tail, pop, or rush into it, either.

CROSSFIRING

I've found that about twenty-five percent of all horses crossfire. This means that they are on one lead in the front end and another in the rear.

If you want a performance horse for classes that call for a lot of flying lead changes, it's best not to start with a crossfiring problem.

The natural crossfiring horse is more common than most people realize. To find out if a horse naturally drops a hind lead, put him in the round pen and move him around it while you are on the ground. If he travels at the canter on the correct lead, but crossfires, then you might think twice about buying him. I am not saying the problem can't be solved, because it can but it takes a lot of work.

THE SEMI-TIRE EXERCISE

This exercise will teach the horse to move only his rear end, on cue. The hardest part of this lesson is getting the horse's front feet in the tire. We'll use a semitrailer tire, with the center smashed down. That way, if the horse catches the bulb of his heel on the tire, we won't have too much of a wreck. If it's a steel-belted tire, make sure there are no loose wires that may cut the horse or get caught between his shoe and hoof.

Sometimes the easiest way to get the horse's feet in the tire is to bring the tire to the horse and carefully lift one front leg while positioning the tire under it. Reassure the horse and then lift the other leg in the tire. Once the horse is standing quietly with both of his front feet in the tire, we are ready to go to the next step.

Using the tire gives the horse a physical barrier to his front feet, while he can easily move his hind feet around it. It will help the horse learn that we want him to take little baby steps around the inside of the tire with his front feet.

To begin, we will stand at the side of the horse, bending his head slightly in our direction while at the same time pushing our fingertips into the spot where our spur would normally hit. When poking the horse, stand up near his head so you don't get kicked. The pressure on his side will cause him to take a step away from us with his hind legs. When he moves, we'll stop and pet him. Do this a few times and then walk around to the other side and repeat the process.

What we are teaching the horse is that pressure in this particular spot means for him to move just his hind end. Our cue is the constant pressure we apply against his side. We don't poke him;

PHOTO: UNA SEELEY

Using a semi's tire gives the horse's front feet a barrier, making it easier for him to move only his hindquarters.

the pressure is steady until he moves away from it. If we put our fingertips into the side of the horse and he doesn't move, then we'll press harder. If he still hasn't moved, then we'll take our hand off his side and come back with a hard poke with our fingers. When we hit him, our hand will not bounce off him, it will stay against his side, again applying constant pressure.

We'll find that if we give the horse the opportunity, he will move on less and less pressure. After just a few minutes of work, the horse will take that one step over with our just brushing the hairs where our spur would hit.

The horse will quickly learn that he is to continue moving his hindquarters until we take the pressure off him. Once he takes one step to the side consistently, then we can begin working on, two steps, then three, and so on until he will go all the way around the tire in both directions. When we stop the pressure, the horse should stop moving.

Practice counting your steps. If you want six, do not settle for seven. If the horse does more steps than you asked for, do not stop him by pulling on him. He is just overreacting and will soon stop taking too many steps on his own.

Another problem we may find is that as soon as we start to the other side, the horse will move away before we ask him to. In this case, we'll keep walking toward him and, when we catch up to him, we'll touch his side where we are giving the cue. We don't want him guessing that we want him to move. Again, he will stop this soon enough, so don't worry too much about it.

Other problems include the horse's crossing his front feet over one another and falling, or falling to his knees, or stepping out of the tire. If this happens, don't jerk on his halter. Just ask him to get up, or to step back inside the tire. Then start over again. He'll soon learn how to take those baby steps, which will keep his legs from crossing.

Once we have mastered the tire exercise ground work (probably in two days of two-hour sessions), then we're ready to go on to the next step.

Put the horse's front feet in the tire and mount him. Begin all over again, asking for just one step left, then one step right. The pressure that had been coming from your fingers while teaching the horse on the ground, will now come from your heel or spur. You will gently press your heel into his side to get his hindquarters to move away from the pressure. Again, as he moves the required number of steps, release the pressure on his side so that he will stop moving. When you get one step on each side, move on to two steps left, two steps right, and so on, until you can ride the horse into the tire and have him step easily all the way around it in both directions.

When working your horse in the tire, be sure to take short breaks periodically so he will not get bored.

SIDEPASSING

The side pass, a lateral movement that occurs when the horse moves his body to the side without going forward or backward, is a logical extension of our semi-tire exercise.

We'll ride the horse out of the tire and ask him to stand still. Now ask him to move only his hind legs to the right, by applying pressure to his left side as described in the tire exercise above. What we want him to do is walk forward. When he starts forward, pick up the reins to stop him. As soon as he stops, release the reins and again ask him to move his hindquarters to the right. When he responds consistently to the cue (pressure), stepping sideways to the right with his back legs, and without moving forward, repeat the exercise in the opposite direction.

When this is accomplished, we'll move on to the next step. Begin to move the horse's rear end to the right, and while it's moving, pick up both reins and ask the horse to step to the right with his front end. Keep your left leg pressure on the horse at the same time. As the horse begins the move forward, pull on the reins until he stops his forward motion. Then release him, but still guide him to the right with the reins. The horse will eventually begin to get the idea.

To perfect sidepassing, practice having the horse move his hind legs only, then both front and rear. Then stop the front leg movement, continuing on with the rear.

Keep the tire around and practice the exercises for at least the next two weeks. Each time you ride the horse, walk him into the tire for a few minutes of practice. Remember to be specific in the number of sidesteps you ask for, because it will become important later in his training.

By practicing these exercises, we will begin to put that first specific spot on the horse's side that, with all the other spots we'll add later, will eventually enable us to throw away our reins.

TEACHING A CUE SYSTEM

In order to have the horse work solely off of our leg commands, a logical cue system must be thought out and taught.

Each cue must be very clear to the horse and he must respond at all levels of performance, excited and calm, in slow work and at high speed. Obviously this is not something you can do overnight with a horse.

There are levels at which results can be seen rather quickly. For example, having your horse work off your legs alone in a small pen. However, it is quite a different matter when you begin to add space, and distractions such as other horses, trail obstacles, and speed. So please be very cautious in how much exposure you give yourself and your horse.

The cue system I use may be completely opposite to yours. Where or how we give the cue is really of little importance. The prime thing is that we are consistent with our cues and that we can control our horse with them.

Keep in mind that the less irritating the cue is to the horse, the longer he will perform the task you are asking him to do without objecting or getting a sour attitude. So keep your cues as soft as possible.

There are quite a few directions a horse can move, and in order to control him, we need to be able to control most, if not all of those directions. That means there are going to be quite a few different cues to teach the horse. The nice part about this is that the horse has as many places to give cues as he has hairs on his body. So you won't run out of places to give cues. Another interesting part of this is that our cue spots do not have to be very far apart. So do not separate your cue spots too much. The horse does not need the separation, and it only pulls you out of a good riding position and off balance. It also does not look very good to your audience.

Since a horse has lots of movements, we need quite an advanced system of cues to completely control him in order for him to do all the different maneuvers when asked.

MY CUE SYSTEM

This is the system my horses are taught. On each side of the horse, we will use four main cue spots. They are the elbow spot, the above-stirrup spot, the stirrup spot, and the spur spot. Each spot can be used alone or in combination with any other spot to teach a specific cue. These cue spots are in addition to those we have used for teaching the walk, trot, and canter.

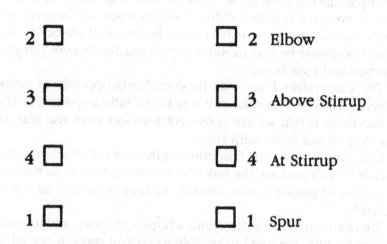

2 ☐   ☐ 2 Elbow

3 ☐   ☐ 3 Above Stirrup

4 ☐   ☐ 4 At Stirrup

1 ☐   ☐ 1 Spur

When teaching these cues, teach one at a time. Make sure the horse understands one very well, before moving on to the next. Whether you plan to ride with or without a bridle, these cues will give you more control over your horse for your own safety.

We taught the first cues during the semi-tire exercise. The horse learned that he was to move only his hindquarters, to the right or to the left, when we applied pressure to the spur (spur, or #1).

The second cue taught is the cue to back up. Both of the rider's feet are brought forward and the rider's toes are wiggled back and forth on the horse's elbows (the elbow, or #2). If you cannot reach your horse's elbows, squeeze and release with both legs several times as you ask the horse to back. Continue this until you want him to stop backing. This is taught after the horse knows how to back in response to the reins.

The next cue spot (the above-stirrup, or #3), is just an inch or two forward from where the stirrup normally hangs, a few inches behind the front cinch. The cue will be given with the heel. It will tell the horse to move his front end around his hind end, either to the right or to the left. Practicing on moving the horse's shoulders in different directions will also help perfect this cue. Direction is controlled by the right or left leg of the rider, as the horse moves away from the pressure that is being placed against him.

The final cue to be taught is given just where the stirrup hangs (at stirrup, or #4). This cue means the horse is to move both his front end and his hind end equally, to the right or to the left, direction again signaled by the rider's leg. This is a direct side-pass manuever. It is a very difficult cue to teach, and requires patience on the part of the rider. For this reason, it should be taught last.

We also have our standard cues to walk, trot, and canter, which have been discussed earlier in the book. They can all be given in their normal places, even if that place seems to you to be directly on top of another cue spot. You will be unconsciously giving a different feel to the horse when you give these cues, and he will be able to tell the difference among them.

These first cues are easy to teach, and anyone who will practice them can teach these, and at least a hundred more, to a horse.

The diagrams that follow show how these cues are used by themselves and combined with others. The black squares show where the cue is given in each case, and the arrows indicate in what direction the horse should move. The number next to each cue spot indicates the order in which it is taught.

HORSE'S HEAD

Imagine the horse's head facing toward the top of the page. The horse's elbows are by the #2 spots. The stirrup hangs straight down, and your spurs touch the #1 spots. The #3 spots are three inches in front of the #1 spots. The #4 spots are taught last.

In the placement of the cue spots, the total space between them is determined by the rider. If you feel a difference between spots #1 and #4, then there is one. Again, cue spots do not have to be far apart for a horse to learn the difference.

MOVING HINDQUARTERS TO THE RIGHT

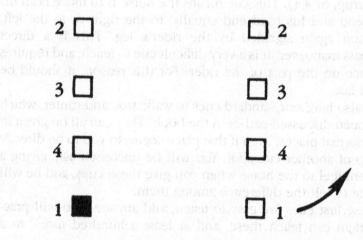

We are moving the horse's hindquarters to the right, while his front legs stay in place. This diagram shows that the cue is given at the #1 spot on the horse's left side.

MOVING HINDQUARTERS TO THE LEFT

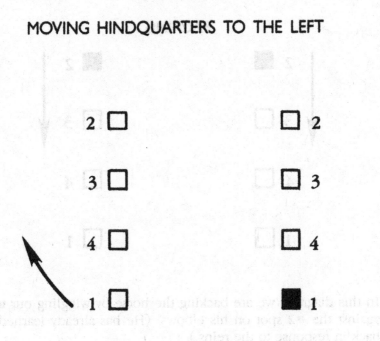

Now we are moving the hindquarters to the left, while the horse's front legs stay in place. The cue is given at the #1 spot on the horse's right side.

BACKING

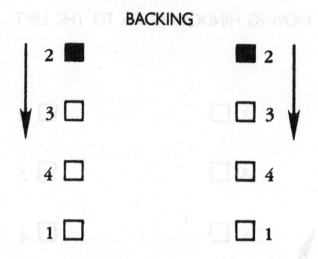

In this diagram, we are backing the horse by wiggling our toes against the #2 spot on his elbows. (He has already learned to back in response to the reins.)

FRONT END TO THE LEFT

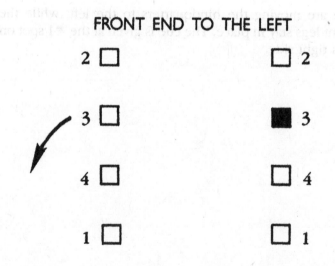

Here we are moving the horse's front end around his hindquarters to the left.

FRONT END TO THE RIGHT

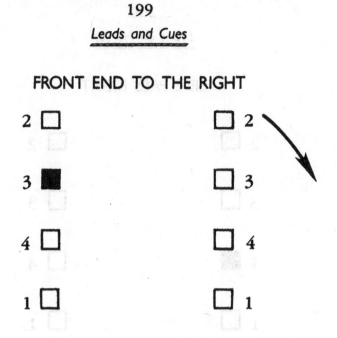

This is the same maneuver as front end to the left, only now we are moving the horse's front end around his hindquarters to the right.

SIDE PASS LEFT

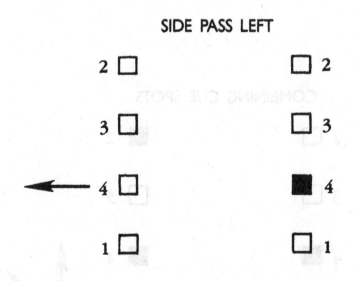

The horse is moving both ends equally to the left.

SIDE PASS RIGHT

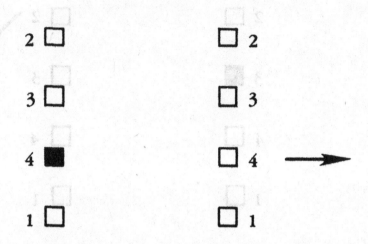

In this diagram, the horse is moving both ends equally to the right.

COMBINING CUE SPOTS

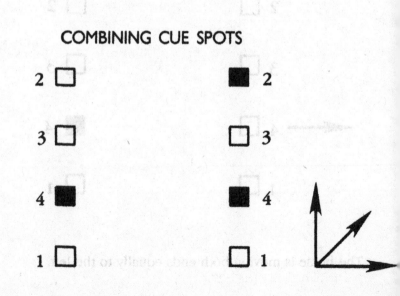

Using a combination of cues, we can have the horse move forward at any diagonal. The #4 spot on the left side would tell him to move right, the #4 spot on the right would tell him to move forward. If he begins to move too much in a straight line forward, then we'll use the back-up cue on the right side (#2) which tells the horse to slow his forward motion.

ANOTHER COMBINATION

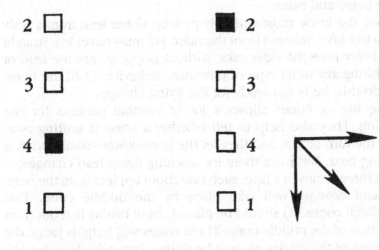

To have the horse move backward and off to the right, we would use the combination of the #4 spot on the left to tell the horse to move both his front end and hindquarters to the right, and the #2 spot on the right to tell him to move backward.

Remember, you don't have to use my cues. You can set up any kind of consistent system that makes sense to you. You may not understand my system, and I may not understand yours, but both of our horses are smart enough to be able to understand what we want. There are no right or wrong cues, just personal signals between our horses and ourselves.

FLYING LEAD CHANGES

In the early clinics, I frequently ran into people who were having problems teaching their horses flying lead changes. The flying lead change refers to a horse's change of lead while cantering. I've tried many quick remedies for solving these problems, from bending horses different ways so as to make it difficult for them to stay in the wrong lead, to ground poles, to changing speeds, as well as other types of training techniques that supposedly fix the problem. I've concluded that the best "fix" is simply correct training. A basic set of rules and exercises will make it easier on both horse and rider.

First, the horse must willingly pick up either lead from a walk and a trot on command from the rider. He must travel in a straight line every time the rider asks, without popping into the lead or exhibiting any other type of unwanted behavior. Until the horse can do this, he is not ready for the flying change.

The use of cones allows a lot of variable patterns for our training. They also help us tell whether a horse is drifting away from the turn or not, and they let the horse know visually what is coming next. We'll use them for teaching flying lead changes.

Set three cones in a line, each one about ten feet from the next. All lead changes will take place by the middle cone. Two additional cones (a) should be placed about twenty feet out from each side of the middle cone. These cones will help us judge the evenness of the circles we will be doing. Two outside cones (b) will be placed twenty feet out from the inside cones (a). The pattern will look like this:

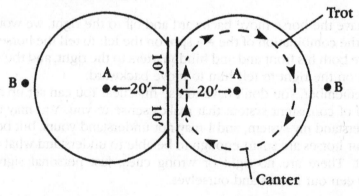

Trot the pattern first, and work only on one side of the center cones. Stay as close to the middle cones as possible and to the inside of the outside cone. Looking at the diagram below, you'll see the pattern we are doing is in the shape of the letter D.

When the horse can trot the D, we are ready to pick up our lead. We will do so only at the middle cone, and we'll be careful not to rush or kick the horse into the lead. We'll squeeze gently, continuing in the lead for half the circle, and then ease the horse back into the trot. This exercise will be repeated for at least ten circles after the horse is doing it perfectly.

Once this is achieved, say from the right, we will then go to the other side of the center cones and practice it from the left. When the horse is doing both sides well, then we will move on to asking for the flying change.

We'll begin by not breaking into a trot in the circles, but by staying in the lope for three or four circles on one side.

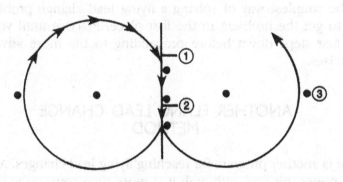

In the diagram above, we are moving clockwise in the left-hand half of the pattern around the cones. When we get ready to make the change, and if we are in the right lead, we'll take the left rein off the horse's neck at cone #1. We will use both reins to straighten the horse up, as this will keep him from dropping his hind lead. We will also look where we are going, to the left, and not at the horse's feet. We'll give the cue for the change by slowly squeezing with our right leg at cone #2. This will result in our riding around just inside the #3 cone, going to the left.

After several passes, the horse will begin to change leads when we just look in the direction we want him to go, and not from the squeezing of our leg. This will keep us from banging him with our legs, thus causing him to speed, or pop up.

It is important that we do not change leads every time we come to the center. Continue loping at least three or four circles on each side before each lead change.

When the horse can do this exercise consistently, it's time to remove the cones and practice the changes in different parts of the arena.

For a western riding pattern type lead change, practice your lead changes in a straight line, without the horse pushing into the bit or into your hands. Don't scare the horse by kicking him with your legs. Elevate the horse's front end just a little, before asking for the change. Do not practice this type of lead change until the horse has the first type down perfectly.

The simplest way of solving a flying lead change problem is not to get the problem in the first place. Practice until you get the first steps down before proceeding to the more advanced exercises.

ANOTHER FLYING LEAD CHANGE METHOD

Here is another program for teaching flying lead changes. Actually, I prefer this one, although it is more time-consuming during training. The system is based on a straight-line approach with cones set at varying distances, say thirty feet between #1 and #2; forty feet between #2 and #3; thirty feet between #3 and #4, and so on. The horse begins at one end of the arena, and always from a stop. This will insure that he is calm and relaxed.

The horse will walk up to the first cone, then trot to the next one, and at the third cone he's to pick up the canter on the right lead. Then back to the trot, to the canter on the left lead, then trot, walk, stop and stand. As the horse becomes better and better at this drill, he will canter more, instead of trotting, between the changes in lead. In this way, the horse can't drop or miss a lead. He'll pick it up no matter what position he is in.

Finally, when we feel confident that the horse is ready to give us a flying lead change when asked, we'll give it a try, eliminating the trotting in the process.

If the horse does not give us the change, we will not deviate from the program. We will go right back to practicing the change, with a little distance done at the trot.

We are trying to teach the horse the cue for taking the correct lead so well that when we ask for it, he gives it to us no matter what gait he is in. So if we ask, and he does not give us the correct lead, we will go back and reinforce the correct canter cue. With practice, there will come a time when we ask, and the horse will give us that change.

There are several good riding habits that we want to maintain during this exercise. First, we do not want to lean over to see if the horse is on his correct lead. We'll look down at our toes if we have to. Whichever of our feet is in front of the other, that is the side the horse is most likely leading on. We'll resist pulling on the reins as we give the horse the cue to change. If the horse begins to rush his change, we will only slow him after he speeds up, not before.

We do not want to ride in a prohibitive manner. What I mean is, if we think the horse is going to make a mistake by rushing the change, and we begin holding him in even before we ask for the change, this is a surefire way to keep the horse rushing into the lead. We'll slow him down only *after* he speeds up, with slow, quiet, gentle hand movements.

Keeping our eyes fixed on an object down the arena, and keeping the horse pointed toward that object, will help us maintain a straight line during our lead changes. We do not want an S-shaped lead change.

When we can successfully complete the flying lead change in this manner, then we're ready to advance to the next series of exercises.

ADVANCED EXERCISES

These exercises consist of ridiog a series of straight lines, with lead changes at particular points in the lines. We will always begin when the horse is stopped, then we'll walk, trot, and canter, asking for a specific lead each time at the canter. We'll end the line in reverse sequence—canter, trot, walk, stop and stand.

The cones will be set along the line at the points where we want the horse to do a change of gait and/or lead. Practicing this way keeps us asking for specifics and lets us grade ourselves. If we miss a cone by three strides, we have found something we need to work on.

The lines should begin easy, with just one change, then progress to many changes on the line. Always use the cones, and bring them closer and closer together, until they are the correct distance apart for a western riding pattern, or about the distance of every other stride for your horse.

Once the horse has mastered this step, we'll spread the cones out to approximately six strides apart. This is an excellent method and one that gives us the best chance at a no-mistakes type of training for the flying lead change. Here are some examples of riding lines for the lead-change training:

CONE
    Stop
    Walk twenty feet
CONE
    Trot thirty feet
CONE
    Canter in right lead sixty feet
CONE
    Trot thirty feet
CONE
    Canter in left lead sixty feet

CONE

    Trot thirty feet

CONE

    Walk twenty feet
    Stop—Stand

CONE

We'll practice this sequence until we're consistently successful, and then we'll cut down the trotting distance between changing leads until flying lead changes are achieved.

Once flying lead changes can be completed, we can go on to the following exercise:

CONE

    Stop
    Walk twenty feet

CONE

    Trot thirty feet

CONE

    Canter right lead sixty feet

CONE

    Lead change; left lead sixty feet

CONE

    Trot thirty feet

CONE

    Walk twenty feet
    Stop—stand

CONE

Again, practice until the horse does this perfectly.

We can keep adding cones until we have the horse changing leads four times in one line. At that point, we'll begin to move the cones closer together in the line, until we're down to two strides between changes.

If we give the cue and the horse picks up the incorrect lead, we will bring him to a stop and ask for the correct lead from a walk. It's important that we do not get angry or jerk or bump him because he made a mistake.

Remember, we do not want the horse scared during any part of the lead-changing training process.

Chapter Fourteen ━━━

Successful
Trailer Loading

A Colorado game warden once told me of a hunter who, after a stint on the mountain, couldn't get his horse back into his trailer to go home. The tired man spent hours trying to load the reluctant animal before he finally closed the trailer door, removed the horse's halter, and turned him loose in the Colorado mountains.

We've all been there. We've been frustrated, angry, scared, embarrassed, and helpless, while the horse we want to trailer remains firmly planted on *terra firma*. Sometimes we can load an unwilling animal, given lots of time, a few friends, butt ropes, blindfolds, tranquilizers, oats, whips, stock trailers, and companion horses. But there are two problems with the above methods. First, they all work some of the time, but there is absolutely no assurance that the horse will consistently go into the trailer. Also, if the horse is unfamiliar with the trailer, he may resist our prodding altogether, no matter what we do.

The second problem is one of safety. Faced with as many methods of trailer loading as there are laggard horses, we will apply the three rules of evaluating a training process to trailer loading. They are important enough to bear repeating here:

1. The procedure must be safe for me. Loading a thousand-pound horse into a box barely big enough to hold him, is fraught with danger. Whatever procedure I use to get my horse into that box isn't any good if I end up crippled, or minus a finger or two.

2. The procedure must be safe for the horse. Again, the technique is of little use if my partner needs his head stitched up, or winds up with a broken leg.

3. The horse must be calmer after the lesson than before it started. I don't need to be wrestling a huge, excited animal into a large piece of metal equipment.

So throughout this procedure we need the horse to be calm. If the horse is afraid and feels trapped in the trailer, he's dangerous to himself and to anyone around him. In order for him to be tranquil in the trailer, he certainly needs to be calm outside of it. If we sedate the horse, he will probably not remember the loading process and will not be any easier to load the next time. So we want the horse's calm awareness to tell us that he understands what we have taught him. His serenity is also insurance that the next time we want him to go into the trailer, he will do so willingly.

As in our other lessons, we need to set goals. Obviously, if the goal is *just* to put the horse into the trailer, we can use the methods we've been using all along. But we'll set a more specific goal for this lesson: *To get the horse into the trailer calmly without either the animal or the handler getting hurt.*

In achieving this goal, we must have other considerations. The trailer cannot be torn up. We also want to be able to load the horse by ourselves. We can't use two people, because we won't always have two people. Also, asking friends for help is not only an imposition, it's dangerous. Any time you have two people working on a fractious horse, trying to get him into a trailer, the odds of someone getting hurt greatly increase.

It's also not safe going into the trailer ahead of the horse, or going into the empty space next to where he will be. We want to release the animal a few feet from the rear door and have him walk calmly past us on up into the trailer.

We don't want any ropes wrapped around anything. They're dangerous and they'll put our fingers in jeopardy. Certainly we will not tie any ropes to, or through, the trailer because we may get trapped between the trailer and the rope.

The horse must stand calmly in the trailer while we put up the butt chain. The animal must also back out of the trailer calmly and slowly when asked.

Finally, and most importantly, we must have control of the horse at all times, because we might make a mistake and need to stop him at any single step while he's going into, or out of, the trailer.

We'll teach our horse to load by setting up the condition often enough and getting the response we want. This is the main difference between loading a horse and teaching a horse to load.

Of course, horses vary a great deal, but the complete teaching process on the worst horse should take no longer than four hours, and our goal can be achieved in as little as ten minutes.

Remember, the horse doesn't know what our goal is, so we can break this process down into stages. If, for some reason, you cannot start and finish the trailering lesson in one day, be sure to end the day's work on a positive note. This way, the horse hasn't had a bad experience, and when you come back the next time, it will not be as hard to get him to the point where you left off. One trainer might do this lesson in a day; another might spread it out over six days.

This method will work one hundred percent of the time and will load every single horse, regardless of his breed, size, disposition, or past experience.

I don't believe in luring a horse into a trailer, so we will not use feed during this lesson. There will be no hay or grain in the trailer because we're not trying to feed the horse, we're trying to teach him to load. We don't use feed when we're teaching him to lead or to sidepass, and we won't use it to teach him to load. Also, anything that distracts the horse—whether it's feed, the cramped quarters, or other people—takes attention away from the trainer.

Most trailer-loading problems originate in leading problems. If you walk up to the trailer and ask the horse to follow you and he does not, but instead stops and stands, or rears, or pulls back, strikes, bites, falls down, or drags you off, your problem is really one of leading, or in this case, lack of leading. With this behavior, the horse leads as long as the trainer is going where the horse wants to go.

We'll begin by teaching a cue for forward movement, so we don't have to get into the trailer with the horse. When a horse moves forward, his hindquarters drive his forehand. In order for the horse to walk up into the trailer, he must first learn to walk past us. The cue we'll set up will mean "move forward." It will be a specific signal that instructs the horse that it's time to get into the trailer. Once the animal learns the cue, it will make no difference whether he is going into a two-horse trailer, a three-horse slant, or a stock trailer.

The cue will not tell the animal to "get into *this* trailer," it will tell him "get into *the* trailer." Teaching him a specific cue to load means that he will respond more effectively and more consistently to our instructions.

The cue at this point in our training will mean just that the horse has to move his feet. Later on in the lesson, it may mean just lean forward, look down, cock a hind foot, or just try. The cue means forward movement. We can decide how much or how little, depending upon the situation. This concept is an extremely important one to understand and to follow. When we are teaching this cue, we'll begin away from the trailer.

We want the horse to learn that when we raise our hand toward his hip, he has to move forward. Eventually it will mean *move forward into the trailer.*

To give the cue, we'll use a stiff dressage whip over which we have complete control. The stiffness of the whip insures that we can stop it in an instant, which is important because timing is critical to this lesson.

We will stand to the horse's left side (the side on which I prefer to stand) close to and in front of his left shoulder, up by his neck. This is also the position we will be in when we are loading the horse into the trailer. Guiding him with our left hand on the lead rope, we'll ask the horse to take a step forward. If he doesn't respond, we'll raise the dressage whip toward his hip. If there is no response, we'll tickle him high on his hip with the tassel on the end of the whip.

Teach a cue for forward movement by tickling or tapping the horse high on the hip with the tip of a dressage whip.

If during the tickling, the horse still does not move forward, we will begin light, slow taps with the whip. The site of the tap is approximately four inches below the tail set, and above the joint of the hip. If you tap down by the hock, the horse will be more apt to kick. He still might kick with the higher taps, but the kicks will be less violent.

When you begin to tap your horse with the whip, do so

extremely lightly. As in the rest of our training, we want to use the least amount of prodding to get the result we seek. The more sensitive the horse is, the less you will have to touch him. Frequently, just a light rub will be enough to get him to move forward. We will increase the frequency and the firmness of the taps until he moves forward. The longer the tapping goes on with the horse not moving forward, the firmer the taps should become, until he does move forward. Even if the final tap is a good, swift hit, get the horse to take a step forward.

Two choices that can't be made during this lesson relate to movement. We can't make the horse stand still, and he can't choose not to move. Keeping this in mind, we'll remember that the horse must move his feet, or show some type of forward motion, such as putting his head down toward the trailer floor, cocking a hind foot, or leaning forward. Forward motion is not always a step forward with the front feet.

If a horse kicks during the tapping, I usually don't reprimand him, as I am up by his neck and in little danger. But if the kicking becomes obnoxious, or it's distracting the horse, or if it's dangerous, then whack the horse below the hock, once for every kick. Hitting below the hock lets the horse tell the difference between the cue up near his tail and a reprimand that tells him we don't want him kicking.

If the horse begins to move backward, increase the taps in speed and firmness. Whenever the horse takes a forward step, immediately stop the tapping and pet him.

Another problem that may show up during teaching this cue is crowding. A little bump the horse gives you here may be magnified later when you are both next to the trailer and he is pushing or smashing you into it. It's important to do what you can to correct such problems while you are still a safe distance from the trailer. A whack below the knees with the whip, or its butt end slapped hard against the horse's side will quickly teach him that crowding is not a reasonable escape. It's very important that we can control the horse whenever we ask him to stop moving, so that he won't run over us.

Once we feel he understands the cue to move forward, generally after ten minutes or so, we'll head for the rear of the trailer, walking with the horse to the point where *he* quits moving.

We'll teach the horse to load on the right-hand, or passenger, side of the trailer. If you are using a ramp-type trailer, stand on the ramp when you get the horse close to the door. By using the right-hand side, there is less chance of getting slammed into an open trailer door. We can switch sides when the horse is going in consistently.

As in our other training, the horse will tell us where we begin our lesson. If he is nervous five feet from the rear of the trailer, this is not the place we'll start. We'll move him back and away from the vehicle, probably a good twenty to thirty feet, to where he is completely relaxed. The distance we are from the trailer is not important. When the horse stops, we stop. And we pet him. The longer we wait here, the better it is, because if we take him closer and he gets excited, he'll know he can return to this spot and relax. This is one of the easiest lessons, for there's a lot of waiting involved.

Try not to become impatient. Wait at least three minutes, or until the horse is completely calm before going on to the next step. It's a good idea to use a watch to help keep track of the minutes. Remember, if you slow down here, you will actually have your horse in the trailer quicker.

After the horse is completely relaxed, again give him the cue to move forward. Raise your hand toward his hip. If he doesn't move forward, tap him with the whip, gradually making the taps firmer until he moves. If the horse begins to back away from the trailer, continue tapping, gradually increasing the number and the firmness of the taps the farther he gets away from the trailer, until he takes a *forward* step.

When he takes that forward step, immediately, no matter how far away from the trailer he is, stop tapping and walk with him toward the trailer. Again, when he stops, you stop and pet him.

The lead rope should be looped around his neck one time, and your hand should be six inches below the snap. This makes it easy to control his nose, the only part of the horse you need to command for this lesson. Don't worry about loading his legs. It's also not important if his rear end is off to one side, for the horse will eventually square up, and the rest of his body will follow his nose. If his nose is at the feed bin in the trailer, it's a good bet that the rest of him will not be far behind.

After a number of forward go-and-stop sessions, we now have the horse's front feet right up next to the back of the trailer.

Think of you, the horse, and the trailer as being on a map. The trailer is at the top of the map, or north. The horse may want to go east or west or south, but he does not want to go north. There is one other direction he can go, and that's up. These are all escape routes, routes he may take to avoid going north, into the trailer. He'll try some, if not all, of these escapes.

If he goes west, he's trying to cut between you and the trailer. As he goes west, his body will smash you into the trailer. If this happens, pop him hard on his hip with the whip. If the horse tries to bowl you over, whip him hard below the knees of his front legs until he stops moving forward.

If he rears up, he'll receive the same treatment—hard whipping below the knees the entire time he's in the air. Remember to always whip below the knees. Whipping above them only encourages the horse to rear, or to rear higher.

If whipping your horse's legs bothers you, put protective gear on them. This makes a fine whopping sound, which will serve to get his attention. We really don't want to hurt him, we'd just like him to remember that awful sound and feeling that he had when he reared on us so he doesn't pursue this type of escape again.

We also don't want to be bitten. If the horse tries to bite, hit him below his knees or on his sides while holding on to the lead rope. His act is so dangerous that I will, in this case, hit him as hard as I can, but only for three seconds. After the three seconds are exhausted, I'll pet him to reassure him I still like him, but again he made a serious mistake that almost cost him his life.

All of these actions are dangerous, so we must be quick and serious about the horse's moving away from us. As we eliminate his escape routes, the only avenue left to him will be north, into the trailer.

If we tap the horse until he takes a step up into the vehicle, we are actually beating him into the trailer and that's not our goal.

At this point, we'll forget about working on the front end, and we'll concentrate our energy on the rear feet. Now we'll have to settle for less movement. Again, the taps don't mean "get into the trailer," they only mean "forward movement." Tap your horse until he leans forward or makes *any* kind of forward movement with his hindquarters. This may be as subtle as the horse's swaying with all four feet on the ground. We don't need an actual step now for movement. All we need at this point is to recognize the thought. Reward forward movement with cessation of the tapping. Pet him.

Remember, our objective is to keep our horse calm and relaxed. The longer we pet him and the longer he stands with his head in the trailer, the more he learns that the trailer is not a bad place to be.

Dropping his head is one indication the horse is thinking about going into the trailer. Get this response and then watch as the weight comes off one hind leg. Before long, when given the tap, he will cock a hind leg. Pretty soon he will take a step forward with one of his hind feet. When we can get him to move it forward and leave it there, then we can begin working on the other hind leg. Keep working at this until the horse will take a step forward with the other hind foot. Eventually he will move both his hind

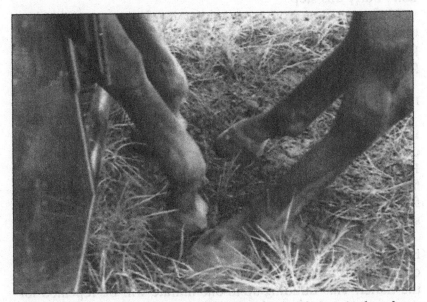

The horse's muscles will quickly tire as his hind feet get closer to his front feet.

feet toward his front feet. The more time taken here, the less likely the horse is to get upset.

As his hind feet keep moving toward his front feet, it becomes harder on the horse's muscles for him to stand in this position for very long. He will become tired, and his hind legs will begin asking his front legs to get into the trailer. Most horses begin to lift a front leg before their hind legs move too far forward.

If the horse moves his hind feet back, ask him again to move them up toward his front feet. Eventually he will pick up one of his front feet and paw, or even step into, the trailer.

The horse may at first paw the trailer floor with one foot. Then he may paw longer and a little slower. Then he may leave the foot on the floor for several seconds.

As one of his front feet steps into the trailer, he'll probably quickly take it out again. Let him. He's learning he can get out of the coffin. Allowing him to go into and out of the trailer at will prevents the horse from feeling trapped. Therefore he stays calm, and we're teaching him to back out of the trailer at the same time we're teaching him to go into it. Every time he backs out, it gives us another opportunity to reteach the cue to get in the trailer, so don't hurry this step.

While any time you are working in close quarters with a thousand-pound animal it's important to watch your feet and his, pay extra attention to this safety consideration while the horse is putting his feet into and out of the trailer.

Repeat the sequence until he will leave his front foot in the trailer for a longer and longer period of time.

If we were to break down the time the horse has one front foot in the trailer into one-minute segments, at the start we'd have one of his front feet in the trailer for five seconds out of the minute. He'd have that same front foot outside the trailer for the remaining fifty-five seconds of the minute. During the fifty-five seconds the foot is outside the trailer, we are petting the horse and letting him stand quietly.

The next step is to reverse the two figures by gradually increasing the time his front foot is actually in the trailer. We'll continue this until his one front foot is spending sixty seconds in the trailer. This building-up-to-one-minute will be repeated for the remaining three feet in sequence. This procedure will not

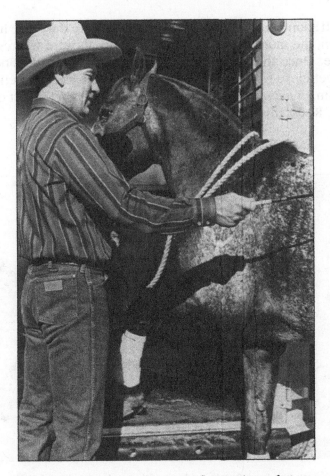

The horse may first paw the trailer floor with one foot.

only help us to be more patient with the horse, but it will also give the horse the repetition of going in and out of the trailer that he will need to become a consistent loader.

Remember, the longer we let the horse stand quietly in the trailer, the more he is learning that it's OK to be there. Let him stand as long as you can before asking for the next step forward.

Now we'll work on getting both front feet in and out of the trailer consistently, calmly, and slowly. Once we get the two feet moving consistently, we'll try for more. With only his two front feet in the trailer, his hind legs are supporting most of his weight and will soon become tired. The longer we leave the horse in this position, the more likely he will be to move forward when given the cue. Once the horse has his front feet in the trailer and his hind feet close to the back of the trailer, we have a tendency to rush him, or even close the door on him to get him the rest of the way in. Resist this temptation.

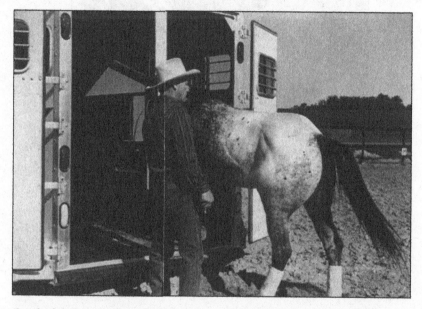

Get the horses's two front feet in and out of the trailer consistently before asking for more.

If you begin to tap and the horse begins to back out of the trailer, keep tapping until he gives you forward movement.

If the horse backs out of the trailer, always have him bring his nose toward you. Doing so keeps his mind on loading, and his body in a position to do so. Remember we need only to control the horse's nose to load him. We do not need to circle the horse to realign him with the trailer, even if his body is at a ninety-degree angle.

The horse may go through this in-and-back-out repetition at

each teaching level. He may put one foot in and then back out of
the trailer twenty times, then both front feet in and out twenty
times, then three of his feet in and out twenty times, before he
finally walks in with all four feet. While some horses will just step
into the trailer with both of their hind feet at once, with no
encouragement, it's better, whenever possible, to have the horse
put three feet in and then back out several times before asking
him to go all the way in.

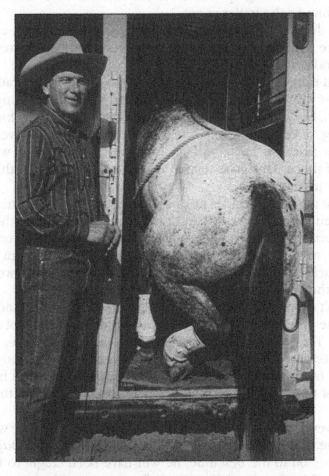

*It's better, whenever possible, to have the horse put three
feet in the trailer before going in the whole way.*

Once the horse has stepped into the trailer once or twice or more, do not insist that he go all the way into the trailer every time. Doing so may scare him and undo some of the work done so far. After ten or more times, we can become more emphatic about his stepping all the way in.

Progress with this method until you have the horse going into and out of the trailer freely. Wait outside the trailer the first few times he goes in all the way. If he comes out, fast or slow, pet him and let him stay out a minute before asking him to go back in. Begin the building-up-to-one-minute method here, but do not close him in the trailer as yet.

The horse will probably go through several stages as you practice loading him. They are: bad, good, real bad, better, half bad, and real good.

He'll start out *bad,* either because he is afraid of the trailer, or because he does not understand what we want. During this session, he will try various escape routes, such as rearing, kicking, striking, or dragging us off. After being taught, and after overcoming his fear, the horse will go into the trailer, or part way in, several times. This *good* section may last anywhere from three to twenty minutes.

Then the horse decides he does not want to go into the trailer at all, even though he has been in it several times. This is the *real bad* section, where he fights hard. He'll try all of his original escape routes, possibly adding a few more, putting extra effort into each one. We'll say "Jiminy Christmas, why didn't we stop when the going was good?"

Don't despair. Continue cutting off each escape route, and then start the procedure over. Begin by asking for one front foot in the trailer. This will be the hardest step to teach at this time, so be prepared and stay calm. The horse will eventually get through his period of resistance. When he does, he will be *better* than he was the first time. He will also be better longer than he was the first time.

However, he is going to have a third bad time. This time will be a halfhearted effort. After he gets through this period of *half bad,* and goes on to the *best* time, he will have been taught to load.

Some horses will go through all these stages of learning, some will not. Most of the horses who have already had bad experiences with trailer loading will go through the full sequence before they are completely trained.

After going through all of the stages of good and bad with the horse, the trainer should be able to walk toward the back of the trailer, let go of the lead rope several feet from the trailer, and watch the horse walk calmly into the trailer on his own.

When the horse will stay in the trailer, walk into the empty trailer stall next to him, pick up the lead rope, give a gentle tug on it, and ask him to back out.

The horse should be comfortable in the trailer before we put up the butt bars or close the door.

After a minute or two, ask him to load again. Repeat this until the horse not only loads easily, but will wait for your cue to unload.

Before we ever put up butt bars or close the trailer door on the horse and lock him in, it is important to accustom him to the banging and slamming we will be doing behind him while he is in the trailer. The best way to teach this is to have him in the trailer with the door on his side open. Bang butt chains and open and close the door on the other (empty) side of the trailer to get the horse used to this racket. In this manner, no harm is done if the horse gets scared and backs out. Once he accepts all of these noises calmly, then he is ready to have his door closed and be hauled safely. Never lock the horse in the trailer until he is comfortable being there.

During the next three or four days, practice this loading method. Be decisive. Look at where you're going, not at the horse. If you're tentative about your horse's getting into the trailer, chances are good he'll be tentative too.

Once the horse has been taught this lesson, you should never have a problem loading him again.

BABY LOADING

It's tempting to want to push or pull a baby into the trailer, especially when he is already halter broken. The problem with this method is that some people, and some colts, will get hurt in the process.

The following technique works on weanlings even if they have not been halter broken, and it keeps them relaxed both in and out of the trailer.

First get the baby to the back door of the trailer. If he is wearing a halter, remove it. You and another person lock hands behind the baby. Do not push him into the trailer. Just stand firm, not allowing him to back away.

The baby will begin looking to the right or to the left for an escape route. When he does, each person should gently guide, or redirect, the baby's nose to the trailer so that he continues looking at it.

When the baby takes a step forward, the handlers should move up with him. Again, do not push forward on him and do not let him back up.

Loading the colt may take ten to fifteen minutes, but he will finally step into the trailer, calm and unhurt.

LOADING THE UNMANAGEABLE OR UN-HALTER-BROKEN HORSE

It's safer to load unmanageable horses or those that are not halter broken, from a distance.

Back the trailer up to the round pen. Move the horse around the pen, in much the same way as we did during our initial round-pen work. Start turning the horse back and forth along the fence. Ask him to turn away from you, not toward you.

Once he turns and stops at your request, ask him to stop in the half of the round pen where the trailer is.

When he stops, make sure that he is facing the trailer. His distance from the trailer is not important, only that he looks at it.

It is important to let the horse rest each time he moves toward the trailer. Once he seems comfortable at each distance, again ask him to move in the direction of the trailer. Accept even one step, then let the horse rest for a minute.

Several times during this stage of the loading procedure, the horse will run by the trailer. When he does this, as quickly as you can, turn him back to the trailer. This will prevent his running all the way around the pen. He is also learning that the only time that he can rest is when he is close to the trailer and looking at it.

Gradually move the horse closer to the trailer until his nose is in the back of it. Every time he takes his nose out of the trailer, make him move, turning him back and forth along the fence.

When the horse is comfortable with his nose in the trailer, ask for more forward movement. He will step into the trailer with his front feet, and eventually his back feet will follow.

If he backs out of the trailer, make him work along the fence before asking him to return to the trailer again. Repeat having the horse go into and out of the trailer several times, until he is comfortable being in it.

Use a rope to close the trailer door. This allows you to be back a safe distance, should the horse kick the door while it is being closed. Open and close the door several times with the rope. At this stage, you can even let the horse back out of the trailer several times before finally locking him in. This will help insure that he accepts being in the trailer and won't hurt himself.

Afterword

I n the beginning of this book, we talked about the importance of defining a problem specifically. We've broken down each problem into a series of small steps, or segment-goals, and worked on each of them in a progressive manner. By setting up a condition and getting a response, we've not only reached our goals, but we now have a horse who is truly a partner.

The last ten years have been fun. They've been filled with a lot of traveling, a lot of teaching and learning, and we've met a lot of nice people along the way. Since those long-ago neighborhood clinics, our program has grown into two-day symposia at horse facilities in major cities across the United States. My hat goes off to all of you who have made this possible.

A special thanks must go to my wife, Susie. She has stood behind me, loved me, and supported me through good times and lean, believing in me every step of the way. Many a midnight before a program would find her on a ladder, hammer in hand, tacking up one last poster for a John Lyons Symposium.

But Susie and I have a special friend who has always been there for us, and I'd like to share with you the important role He has had in our lives.

When we started in the clinics, we were at a financial crossroads in our lives. We were struggling with the ranch, which we loved, but the economic prospects for continuing were pretty grim. We had the idea for the clinics, but we both knew that it would take time before they would support us. Also, if they were successful, it would mean that I would be gone from home a great deal of the time.

We decided to do our best to turn our lives, and the business, over to God and let Him direct us.

I can honestly tell you that there were many times when we didn't have enough money to buy gas to go to the next clinic. En route, I'd call the host, and he or she would tell me there weren't any horses signed up. Many times it looked as though there was just no way we could continue. But then we would both pray for God's help, and He never let us down. He continually saw us through those rough times.

Quite often at night, while on the road, I'd reread comments from symposium participants over and over, and these folks would keep saying to me that there was a need, and that God was involved with us.

God has stood by me and my family. I can't begin to tell you of all the miracles He has done for us. While I am by no means the best example of a Christian, I wanted to take this opportunity to tell you all that I believe with all of my heart that God is real, and that He will help you with your everyday lives, just as He has helped us with ours.

Finally, thanks to all of you who have had the patience and interest to sit down and read *Lyons on Horses*. Good luck to you in your training.

God bless and keep you.

John Lyons